STRIKE
A STUDY OF CONFLICT

STRIKE

A STUDY OF CONFLICT

SUKANTI PRIYA PATTNAIK

GYAN

GYAN PUBLISHING HOUSE

NEW DELHI-110 002

ISBN : 81-212-0445-3

Library of Congress Card No. 93-900302

Published in 1993 by
Gyan Publishing House
5 Ansari Road
New Delhi - 110002

Composed by Ideal Computers Pvt. Ltd., Delhi-110007
and
Printed at Goyal Offset Works, Delhi

CONTENTS

ACKNOWLEDGEMENTS

I would like to acknowledge my debts to my supervisor, Dr. Abhay Kumar, Professor, Department of Labour Welfare, Utkal University who has supervised the research work and also inspired me to write this book. My revered teachers Dr. Bidyadhar Mishra, noted economist of the State and Ex-Vice-Chancellor of Utkal University and Prof. Gopal Chandra Rath, Retd. Professor Department of Industrial Relations and Personnel Management, Berhampur University for their encouragement, and Dr. B. Ranganathan, Principal, Nachuni College who has gone through the manuscript of this book. I am also grateful to Prof. J. Pattnaik, Department of History, Utkal University for his valuable suggestions.

I would like to thank my younger brothers Sabhransu and Snehansu who assisted me in the preparation of the manuscript.

S.P. Pattnaik

FOREWORD

I had the pleasure of going through the book, "Strikes–A Study of Conflict" by Dr. (Miss) Sukanti Priya Pattnaik. The book contains an analysis of various aspects of industrial conflicts in Orissa, an industrially backward state of India. In modern industrial systems, conflicts between labour and management are inevitable. They are inherent features of modern industries. Though labour and management have common interest in the growth, prosperity and efficient management of industries, they have divergent interests in many vital matters, like payment of wages, sharing of profits, maintenance of proper conditions of work and promotion of labour welfare. The degree of participation of labour in management and sharing powers in decision making are also areas of conflicts.

In all modern large-scale industries, labour has been highly organised and is in a position to take part in management and decision making through its unions. Differences in interests and views and lack of understanding and communication gaps breed conflicts between labour and management and cause various problems and dislocation in industries. Conflicts and stoppage of work hampers the growth of industries and effect the interests not only of labour and management but also of the whole society. Conflicts particularly in industries producing essential goods and services cause great loss, inconvenience and suffering to the whole community. As such, not only labour and management but also the whole community has a stake in the smooth working of industries.

In all modern societies, therefore, governments take various legal and administrative measures to ensure smooth working of industries and minimise conflicts in the interest of all sections of the society. For efficient industrial administration and promotion of harmonious growth of industries, knowledge and understanding of the conditions of industries, problems of labour and management in them, causes of conflicts and effective ways to minimise them are essential. Stages and conditions of industrial development, causes of conflict and possibilities of their elimination are not same in all countries, regions or industries. In-depth studies in different industries in different regions are necessary.

In this study an analysis of the nature and problems of industrial conflicts and occurrences of strikes in an industrially backward region has been presented which is of interest not only to the administrators and planners of the region but to all scholars in the subject. The author has surveyed the trends in strike activities in manufacturing and non-manufacturing industries in the public and private sectors in the state over a period of about three decades and examined their causes. She has analysed the distribution of strikes by causes and sizes of plants and has studied the impact of size of plants on the strikers' participation rates. She has also studied the inter-industry propensity to strike, durations of strikes, the role of unions and labour groups in the organisation of strikes and the manner in which strikes have been terminated.

In general, she finds that in Orissa, industrial development and trade union movement started late. Even today the number of large scale industries and the number of workers employed in them are small in comparison of other states of India. With increased factory employment and unionisations, naturally industrial disputes and work stoppages have increased. About ninety percent of the work stoppages occurred due to strikes by workers and ten percent due to lockouts. During the last three decades, the frequency of strikes, workers' involvement and loss of man-days have shown increasing trend. The rates of increase have been much higher than the All India average. In comparison to the number of labourers employed, the number and percentage of strikes in manufacturing industries were higher than in non-manufacturing industries. The degree of unionisation in the manufacturing sector was also higher than that in the non-manufacturing sector. Unionisation increased both in the public and private sectors and increased unionisation had positive impacts on striking activities in both the sectors. But only about five percent of the total number of plants were affected by strike activities, ninety five percent of the plants were unaffected.

Generally strike activities were concentrated in large sized plants. The larger the plant, the greater is the probability of strikes and strike activities imposed a greater burden in terms of loss of man-days in larger plants than in small sized plants. But worker participation rate in strikes was lower in larger sized plants than in smaller sized plants. Strikes in smaller sized plants lasted longer than in larger sized plants. Strikes in large plants were mostly departmental, general strikes being very small in number. Large sized plants were multi-union plants while small plants generally did not have more than one union. Worker militancy and duration of strikes were greater in small plants than in large plants.

With regard to causes of strikes, economic issues were the most important causes accounting for about 55 percent of the strikes and 60 percent of the man-days lost. In economic issues pay increase was the issue in about 60 percent of the strikes. This was natural in the context of inflationary trend during the whole period of study. Personnel issues were the next important cause and it was noticed that importance of such causes was increasing. There was positive linkage between cost of living index and strike activities on wage issues. Nature of demand and size of the organisation greatly influenced participation rates. The participation rates were naturally much higher in strikes on economic issues than on personnel issues. As economic issues were the most important cause of strikes both parties, labour and management, were anxious to terminate the strikes as quickly as possible to avoid loss. Therefore two-thirds of the strikes were settled in less than five days. Duration of strikes was also short as conciliation mechanism was able to play an effective role in settlement of conflicts. As the state is not industrially developed, rate of unionisation was not high. The majority of the unions were small and independent organisations not affiliated to All-India unions. Forty to fifty percent of the strikes were not declared by unions but by small workers' groups. Multi-union plants were more prone to strikes. In the state however, though the frequency of strikes is increasing, about 95 percent of the plants were strike free. In terms of duration of strikes and participation rates of labourers, industrial conflicts do not pose a serious threat to industrial growth at present. Only some industries like electricity and transport have become very strike prone.

In general the book gives a comprehensive analysis of various aspects of industrial conflicts and strike activities in Orissa and indicates the regional peculiarities. I believe, it will be useful to industrial administrators, labour leaders and all persons interested in subjects like industrial relations, personnel management and labour welfare.

B. MISRA
Former Professor of Analytical & Applied
Economics and Former Vice-Chancellor of the
Utkal University

Bhubaneswar

PREFACE

The growing concern over the frequent occurrence of strikes and its tendency to increase, insisted this author to research out data available for the industrial sector in Orissa. The research in this report is designed to provide a framework to understand the nature and extent of strike activity in the State in particular and in the country in general.

In industry workers' discontentment with his material and other conditions of life breeds conflict. Most of the conflicts arose from the organised efforts of working people to improve their lot. They use different pressure tactics upon the management to attain their objectives and strike is the last resort. So strike is a group action mobilized by the social process to exert pressure upon the management.

Strike as a form of industrial conflict can be expressed in many ways, strikes can be analysed in their own right. A study of strike pattern is not a substitute for detail examination of the various ways in which conflict is expressed, but it has the advantage of concentrating on behaviour which is undoubtedly conflict and which is conceptually distinct from other actions.

The findings of the study prove to be an aid to the understanding of the problem. It seeks answers to the rising trend of strike statistics. There is concentration of strikes in certain industries and in certain plants. Most of the plants are free from industrial stoppages. Even within the strike affected industries there are many strike free plants. The result of the study shows that strike activity and plant size is positively related. The analysis support the findings of other scholars that economic interest of the workers explain much about the conflict between labour and management. The study also proves that positive relationship exists between degree of unionisation and strike activity. The nature of strike demand is the main motivating factor of strikers' participation in strikes.

The results of the report would prove to be useful for careful examination of several questions, for example, why rate of participation in strikes is high in few plants while the vast majority of plants remain relatively unaffected. It is also hoped that the socio-psychological analysis of strike action would stimulate further thinking and research in future to discover the process of mobilization of strike action. It is through the use of the case study, particularly that an attempt can be made to explain the behaviour of the participants in strike situation. The case study of a strike-prone organisation may serve to explain the sociological process involved in a strike action.

INTRODUCTION

Labour and Management compose an important and integral part of our industrial society. The very framework of our industrial society has created an atmosphere where both these groups work as pair of opposites, their interests clash at some point or other. But at the same time they have some common goal, namely the preservation of the organization. Despite all the emphasis laid by social scientists on the common goal and the virtues of industrial harmony conflict has become an inherent feature of modern system of production. Between conflict and cooperation, conflict is the more common and also delicate and unless handled with utmost care it may lead to open warfare between two organized groups, viz, labour on the one hand and management on the other thus stifling growth. Hence it occupies a prominent place. Constant efforts are being made to minimise if not mitigate such conflict and to preserve smooth labour- management relations and to develop mechanisms acceptable to both the groups to deal with such group conflict. It may not be out of place to mention here that industrial conflict should not be constructed as equivalent to the use of violence. While violence does occur on some occasions, it is unusual rather than a common feature of labour-management conflict.

The problems of industrial conflict are not new. They have bedeviled labour-management relations in the history of modern system of production. The past has witnessed many intense and sometimes violent industrial disputes. These conflicts arose from the organised efforts of the working people to improve their economic and social conditions. True, the working people had to face stiff resistance from employers, who in order to curtail the powers of the trade unions, used instruments of the government on the plea of maintenance of law and order or protection of public interest. Many times extra-constitutional measures were also adopted to weaken them. Even the judiciary, based on the old concept of common laws, was utilized to weaken the organised strength of the working class. This struggle of organised working class to acquire legal right to organize and bargain collectively with employers continued fairly long.

In spite of these bitter conflicts between labour and management, many employers during these years succeeded in maintaining smooth labour-management relations and improved wages and working conditions without labour resorting to strikes. The Tata Iron & Steel Company in Bihar has not witnessed a single major strike during the last 50 years. So also is the case of Aska Sugar Co-operative (Orissa), where no strike has occurred during the last 20 years.

Important changes have occurred in labour-management relations during the last four decades. Labour is more organised and wields enormous power not only on employers but also on government. Trade Unions have succeeded in getting enormous legislative protection and have prevented the government machinery and even the judiciary from adopting a pro-management approach. Not less significant than organised labour's growth is the remarkable change which has occurred in the attitude of management and even the general public. Management today is not the enemy of trade unions, rather it has learnt to live with it. Public opinion is also now not opposed to unionism. As a result of these changes, the sense of despair on the part of labour is fast disappearing.

Notwithstanding these changes, conflict between labour and management is common and often results in violence, inflicting intolerable hardships on society. Now both the groups have become so organised that each wields enough influence to keep from being 'pushed around' and could very well stifle the pace of economic growth and also hold society to ranson. No developing nation which has set before herself the task of economic development through planned economic efforts could allow rough employer- employee relations to prevail. In this developmental process, any factor which retards growth or upsets the plans for development is viewed as socially non-functional. Strikes not only impede the continuous flow of goods and services, but also upsets the timing of these flows and the pattern of expectations warranted by such flows. This is why it is often said that economic progress is bound up with industrial harmony.

Orissa which is one of the poorest states in India, having a per capita income of Rs. 1983.00 in 1987-88 as compared to all India average of Rs. 3284.00 at current prices,* has joined other states in the task of economic development to raise the per capita income of the people. But economic progress is bound up with industrial harmony. Industrial harmony, inevitably requires faster co-operation between employers and employees. Such co- operation leads to increased productivity and all round improvement of the country. Thus, healthy industrial relations on which industrial harmony is founded, can't be regarded as a matter exclusively for employers and employees; it is of vital significance to everyone who is interested in peace, stability and economic prosperity.

OBJECTIVES

It is against this background that the present study has been taken up. This study aims at analysing the present day industrial conflict in the State of Orissa in a comprehensive manner, covering the nature and meaning of strikes, their causes and conditions and the attempted methods for reducing and dealing with them. The treatment is analytical rather than descriptive so as to provide an insight and understanding into the problems of industrial conflicts rather than to offer procedures or formulas for reducing industrial conflicts.

---

* *Source* : Economic Survey, Government of Orissa, 1989-90.

HYPOTHESIS

Propounding theoretical arguments on the nature of strike activity, this study intends to provide insight into the important dimensions of the problem. A set up of hypothesis based on the findings of eminent scholars like Ross and Hartman,[1] Knowles,[2] Albert Rees[3] and others are formulated to measure the intensity and magnitude of the problem in Orissa. In particular, the study aims at testing the under mentioned hypotheses:

(1) Are strikes withering away over the years? (Ross & Hartman)[4]

(2) Are economic causes still predominant or have they given place to non-economic causes like personnel issues? Again, among the economic causes, is higher pay the main rallying cry of the industrial workers?

(3) Is there any relationship between strike activity on the one hand and factors like cost of living index and average annual earning on the other?

(4) Is strikers, participation dependent or independent of the nature of strike demand?

(5) Does cohesiveness among workers in strike actions depend on the size of the plant ?

(6) Are the larger plants having greater propensity to declare frequent strikes?

METHODOLOGY AND SCOPE

At the outset it is proposed to examine the views on the meaning and the right to strike and their legal implications in Britain, U.S.A. and India. The literature developed on the subject in the national and international context is obtained from national and international journals and books, and some of the important findings are proposed to be critically examined in the current study. On the basis of a theoretical framework an attempt is made to arrive at an empirical analysis of the data collected from the official records of the Labour Directorate, Orissa, the Chief Inspector of Factories, Rourkela Steel Plant and Published Literature of the Bureau of Statistics, Orissa, Labour Bureau, Simla, Trade Union Records, etc.

The trend of industrial disputes and work-stoppages due to strikes and lock-outs is analysed for three decades (1960-89) and wherever necessary a comparative picture of India and Orissa is given. In the absence of systematic data prior to 1964 on details of strikes, like cause, duration, method of settlement, union involvement, inter-industry propensity to strike, nature of strike-affected organisations, etc., the current study concentrates on the period between 1964 and 1989 for detailed examination of the problem.*

CHOICE OF MEASURE OF STRIKE ACTIVITY

The seriousness of strike is measured either in terms of numbers of strikes or workers involvement ratio or man-days lost. But none of these measures individually will give a true picture of the magnitude of a strike. Take for example, strike frequency. Strike frequency reflects the outbreak of industrial conflict rather than its magnitude. The figures on aggregate strike numbers give the same weightage to a one-day stoppage involving ten workers as to a general strike in an industry causing the loss of thousands of working days.

Therefore, eminent scholars like Vanderkamp,[5] Walsh,[6] Galambos and Evans[7] have contrary views on accepting a single measure of strike activity. While Vanderkamp accepts statistics of working days lost as the most comprehensive single measure of strike activity, Walsh holds the view that the working days lost figures may not be affected significantly, if the duration of stoppages rise with the decline in the number of strikes. Thus he does not accept the statistics of working days lost as the most comprehensive single measure of strike activity.

Faced with this problem of choice, Galambos and Evans constructed a common index for strike activity by calculating the arithmetic mean of these three measures without assigning any weightage whatsoever. They argued that any effort at apportioning weightages for these different measures should be precisely stated. This index was not intended to measure the hardship, loss of output, damage to the economy or any other of the possible consequences of stoppages. It was only meant to show changes in the level of strike activity.

* Strikes involving even less than 10 workers and lasting less than a day are also included.

This approach which has not been adopted by other researchers like Walsh and Knowles is open to criticism mainly on one count i.e., in the analysis of strike activity it is not pure numbers that one is looking for, but also their implications. Without any consideration of such implications, the phenomena would be reduced to mere abstraction which may have very little research value. Thus, a more pragmatic approach would be to analyse the strike activity from different dimensions applying all the three measures, viz., number of strikes, number of workers involved, and working days lost.

The current study relies on Knowles's statement and analysis including each of the above mentioned three components of strike activity. An attempt has also been made to measure the relationship of these three measures with one another to see how far one represents the other.

A few other secondary indices, like the average size of strikes (number of strikers divided by number of strikes), the average duration (days lost per striker), etc., are also analysed to measure the different dimensions of strike activity. Statistical methods like correlation co-efficient and least square method have also been used for analysis.

This study is based on macro-level analysis and it is limited to the organised sector, and wherever necessary a comparative picture of strike activity in Orissa and India is given.

PLAN OF THE STUDY

The structure of the study-report is designed in a systematic manner to provide a clear picture of the problem. The report begins with the discussion of the background of the problem, the scope, the objective and methodology adopted, and limitations of the research project. In the discussion, it is considered useful to provide a brief summary of the study and findings in a planned way.

To begin with, Chapter I explains the meaning and definition of strike in the light of the definitions of different authors and legislative enactments of different countries. The chapter gives special attention to the discussion of "Right to strike". While referring to the history of trade union movement in countries like

Britain, U.S.A. and India, the struggle of the working class to obtain this precious right is described. The views of eminent scholars like G.D.H. Cole, Chamberlain on the right to strike are critically examined for the deeper understanding of the problem. Court verdicts and legislative provisions on this controversial issue are also discussed in detail. Specific discussions on the case laws developed in India on this issue are utilized to give a historical perspective of the problem.

Chapter 2 highlights the literature developed on the subject at national and international level. The findings of eminent scholars like Ross and Hartman, Knowles, Albert Rees, Kerr-Siegel and others in the international field and the studies of V.B. Karnik, Promod Verma, Iswar Dayal and Sharma at the national level are discussed at length and their arguments and counter- arguments are examined to give a wider perspective to the examination of strike activity in Orissa.

Chapter 3 contains the background statement of strike activity in Orissa. In providing a picture of the industrial climate of the state, an attempt is made to examine the trend of industrial disputes and work-stoppages due to strikes and lock- outs during the 1960's and the 1970's. The trend of each component of strike activity like frequency, workers involved, man-days lost is analysed and examined through statistical analysis. Distribution of strikes in public and private sectors, manufacturing and non-manufacturing sectors, and different industries is also discussed to give a clear picture of the problem. The growth of trade unions during the same period is also analysed with the object of establishing the relationship between growth of trade unionism and strike activity.

An attempt has been made in Chapter 4 to analyse the relationship between strike activity and plant size. The various plants have been classified into five categories according to their magnitude of employment. An attempt has been made on the basis of strike data for a period of three years (1978-80) to establish the relationship between strike frequency and plant size.

The causative factors have been examined in Chapter 5. Specific discussions are introduced on the economic and non-economic reasons of strike, referring to the trend over the decades.

Factors like rise in the cost of living index, earnings of workers etc. are examined to ascertain their impact on strikes on economic issues. Their co-relation is established through statistical analysis. Workers, response to the strike call on different causes and in different types of organisations is also examined in minute detail in this chapter.

Chapter 4 deals separately with the other important dimensions of strikes in Orissa. It analysis the inter-industry propensity to strike, duration of strikes, length of strikes, union involvement and the methods employed to restore normalcy.

In the concluding chapter, an attempt is made to provide a resume of previous chapters. It looks into the findings of different studies discussed in Chapter 2 and critically evaluates the findings of the current study.

LIMITATIONS

Owing to the non-availability of all the necessary data over a long period, a long term industrial trend could not be studied which might otherwise have yielded a clearer picture of the problem. The unemployment figures of industrial workers are also not available, for which reason the general unemployment figures have been used for the purpose of this study. Similar difficulty was experienced in obtaining the real wage rates of industrial workers. Employment figures of each industrial organisation is not available for a long period from which the rate of participation in strike activity can be studied. This analysis is therefore restricted to a three year period i.e. 1986 to 1988. The unavailability of figures for union membership for each organisation for the period under study, created difficulty in studying the impact of unionisation on strike activity. Data on the results of strikes are also not available making it impossible to measure the strength of unions in strike. Details of illegal strikes are difficult to get to evaluate the nature of strikes.

Barring the above mentioned limitations, the present study aims at examining the various hypothesis stated in one of the preceding pages of this chapter.

NOTES

1. Arther M. Ross and Paul T. Hartman. 'Changing Patterns of Industrial Conflicts', Wiley, 1960, p.8.

2. K.G.J.C. Knowles. 'Strike-Proneness and its Determinants', in Walter Galenson and Seymour Martin Lipset (ed.) Labour and Trade Unionism, Wiley, 1960, pp. 301-18.
3. Albert *Rees*. 'Industrial Conflict and Business Fluctuations,' Journal of Political Economy, Vol. 60 No. 5 Oct. 1952, pp. 371-82.
4. Arther M. Ross and Paul T. Hartman. 'Changing Patterns of Industrial Conflict,' Wiley, 1960, p. 42.
5. J. Vanderkamp. 'Economic Activity and Strikes in Canada,' Industrial Relations, (California), Vol.9. No. 2 Feb. 1970, pp. 215-30.
6. W.D. Walsh. 'Economic Condition and Strike Activity in Canada,' Industrial Relations, (California), Vol. 14, No. 1, Feb. 1975, pp. 45-54.
7. Galambos and Evans. 'Work-Stoppage in United Kingdom, 1951-64 : A Quantitative Study', Bulletin of the Oxford University Institute of Economics and Statistics, Vol. 28, No. 1, 1966, pp. 33-67.

2. K.G.J.C Knowles, 'Strike Proneness and its Determinants', in Walter Galenson and Seymour Martin Lipset (eds.) Labour and Trade Unionism, Wiley, 1960 pp. 301-18

3. Albert Rees, 'Industrial Conflict and Business Fluctuations', Journal of Political Economy, Vol. 60 No. 5 Oct. 1952 pp. 371-82

4. Arthur M. Ross and Paul T. Hartman, Changing Patterns of Industrial Conflict, Wiley, 1960 p. 62

5. J. Vanderkamp, 'Economic Activity and Strikes in Canada', Industrial Relations (California) Vol. [illegible] No. 2 [illegible] pp. 215-30

6. W.D. Walsh, 'Economic Conditions and Strike Activity in Canada', Industrial Relations (California) Vol. 14 No. 1 Feb. 1975 pp. 45-[illegible]

7. John Pencavel, 'An Investigation into Industrial Strike Activity in Britain', Economica [illegible]

[illegible] Gilbert and Evans, 'Work Stoppages in United Kingdom, 1951-64 : A Quantitative Study', Bulletin of Oxford University Institute of Economics and Statistics, Vol. 28, No. 1, 1966 pp. 32-47

1

STRIKE-AN OVERVIEW

MEANING OF STRIKE

Industrial conflicts find expression in various forms like industrial disputes, work-stoppages through strikes and lock-outs, bandhs, gheraos, restrictions of output, sabotage, machine breaking, demonstration, pamphlet writing, etc. Of these, strikes and lock-outs are most conspicuous. The strike is a temporary suspension of functions. Strike involves a refusal by a body of workers to obey orders and to perform duties assigned to their jobs. It is a concerted protest action. There is no unanimity among social scientists over the meaning of strike. While the Encyclopaedia Britannica defines strike as a concerted refusal to work under conditions required by employers, Knowles views strike as a collective stoppage of work undertaken to bring pressure to bear on those who depend on the sale or use of the products of that work. A somewhat similar definition has been given by Schneider, who defines strike as a concerted and temporary suspension of functions designed to exert pressure upon others within the same social unit. All these definitions consider withdrawal of labour as strike. Restrictive practices like go-slow are not covered by these definitions. Albert Rees, on the other hand, defines strike in a manner which by implication includes go-slow, within the meaning of the term strike. According to him, strike means planned withholding of labour designed to impose union demands on the employer or to prevent the employer from imposing his demands on the union.

The British Industrial Relations Act (1971) defines strike as concerted stoppage of work by a group of workers in contemplation or furtherance of an industrial dispute, whether they are parties to the dispute or not, whether in the case of all or any of these workers, the stoppage is not in breach of the terms and conditions of their employment and whether it is carried out during or on the termination of their employment. The U.S.A. Labour Management Relations Act of 1947 also defines strike as concerted stoppage of work by employees or any concerted slow down or other concerted interruption of operations by employees. The Indian Industrial Disputes Act of 1947 defines strike as cessation of work by a body of workers employed in any industry, acting in combination, or a concerted refusal under common understanding, of any number of persons who have been so employed to continue to work or to accept employment .

A brief review of the above definitions would thus reveal that temporary but concerted suspension of work by the workers is an important feature of strike and this suspension aims at exerting pressure on employers to agree to their terms and conditions.

RIGHT TO STRIKE

The 'Right to Strike' plays a significant role in the power struggle between labour and management. To match the great powers of capital, unions evolved different tactics—to pressurise both employers and government—the two chief participants in the power structure. Strike is the most spectacular of all labour tactics by which an organised group displays its strength against the management.

Experience all over the world shows that strikes are inevitable in an industrial society. Strikes are commonly used to exert economic pressure, and are intended to hurt business, or to strain relationships so that normal functions are brought to a halt, or at least inhibited. The strike is regarded as a legitimate and powerful weapon in the hands of workmen in dealing with an employer who refuses to accept their demands. However, strikes are in themselves economically wasteful and cause hardship. "Strike is neither an act of war against industry nor against an employer. It is basically a weapon of self-defence against the arbitrary and unjust policy of the management. Strike, therefore, is a social necessity for promoting or defending a just economic interest of the working class."

According to G.D.H. Cole, "workers are required to resort to strike because basically there is no equality between them and their employers.... Employers and workmen may be, in the eyes of the law, equal parties in fact. The workman under contract is bound to serve his employer; the employer is entitled to order the workman about the relation between them is essentially unequal."

The National Commission on Labour in India (1969) has recommended that the state must recognize the fundamental fact that the strike phenomena is a necessary concomitant of the present industrial culture; the employers must accept that trade unions are an important ingredient of the industry without which industry cannot run efficiently.

The Royal Commission on Labour in India (1931) has also remarked: "Strike ban is no panacea for conflicts. There can be no mathematical formula of calculation, addition or subtraction in industrial jurisprudence to contain social forces and processes within a society which call for a new change in its moral and material philosophy. The problem is basically human which transcends differences of social systems. We should not seek to impose any rigid patterns for the fear of strike which otherwise would impede the growth of independent trade unionism vital for the establishment of industrial democracy."

The views of different authors mentioned above agree that strike is essential to the union's survival. The workers must have the freedom to refuse to sell or to withdraw their labour. In a free society, if the citizens are allowed the freedom of speech, of press, and of assembly, it is inevitable that the workers should agitate for the removal of their grievances and improvement of their conditions; and the agitation may on occasions lead to strikes. The strike is treated as a basic human right which can only be abolished along with all other fundamental rights. But it is difficult to suggest whether the workers should be allowed to enjoy unrestricted right to strike or some restrictions should be imposed by legislation or convention or through agreements freely negotiated between workers and employers. Workers cannot be granted unrestricted freedom to stop any kind of work at any time they like. Certain types of work have to be carried on uninterrupted if society is not to be paralysed and disrupted. But society cannot be allowed to run smoothly at the cost of the interest of workers engaged in those activities. In order that there might be no social disruption, the workers should be adequately paid and their interest should be properly protected. The American Federationist, the official journal of the AFL-CIO rightly pointed out that the strikes are never welcomed by society and seldom desired by industry or labour but they become necessary for promoting general welfare and establishing justice for workers. It, inter-alia, states:

"The right to strike is inseparable from human freedom. No genuine democracy will consider outlawing strikes."

Again, the strike is viewed as an essential ingredient of collective bargaining. In the words of Allan Flander, where negotiation, i.e. "diplomatic use of power," fails, collective action or the threat of such action is the power with which unions achieve or hope to achieve their demands.

To quote O. Kahn-Freund, "collective bargaining as we understand it is unthinkable without social sanctions. By this we mean that neither an employer nor a trade union can bargain effectively or hope to enforce the observance of collective agreements, unless there is in the background the possibility of using economic and social pressure against the other side of the bargaining..... collective bargaining cannot work without the ultimate "sanction" of the strike and the lock-out, no more than the law of say, the sale of goods could work without the law of bankruptcy."

A somewhat similar view is held by Sinha and Sinha. They hold the view that it is the fear of strikes that induces an employer to agree to the terms demanded by the union. Similarly, it is the fear of lock-outs that keeps the union in a reasonably accommodating frame of mind. Even when the terms and conditions have been peacefully negotiated, it is the threat of strikes and lock-outs, apart from any moral obligations on the parties concerned to abide by the terms of settlement, that prevents the parties from deviating from the mutually accepted course of action.

After considering the views of different authors, Chamberlain says:

"To those who regard collective bargaining as a marketing procedure involving the sale of labour services, the strikes and lock-outs, for example, may be upheld as necessary to a freedom not to contract, as an alternative to a forced sale purchase. On this ground, limitations on these rights might be opposed in principle. On the other hand, those who look upon the bargaining process as the basis of a group Government or as a method of management, might on this ground, conclude that strikes and lock-outs as instruments of bargaining power are not necessary in principle even if unavoidable at the present."

The above discussion makes it abundantly clear that the right to strike raises many controversial issues. A review of labour legislations of different countries would reveal that almost all the countries have put restrictions in one form or another on strike activity. Legislative measures alone may not prevent workers from making use of their right to strike. The communist countries, where legislation is very restrictive in controlling strikes, also face at times the problem of strike. The recent agitation by workers in Poland is an example of the inadequacy of legislative measures in preventing workers from resorting to strike.

The history of labour movements in countries like U.K., U.S.A. and India throw some light on this controversial issue. A study of different occasions where the workers were paralysed for their strike activity, reveals the interesting fact that collective action has only encouraged them to proceed further for strengthening the trade union movement.

RIGHT TO STRIKE IN GREAT BRITAIN

The history of strikes in Great Britain is closely linked with the history of the trade union movement. The Industrial Revolution came first in Britain, resulting in the establishment of a number of factories and the employment of labour. The growth of factory employment gave rise to trade unionism and adoption of different pressure tactics by the labourers to counter the powers of the employer. Of the various pressure tactics adopted by trade unions the strike was probably the most effective. The efforts of workers to combine and form unions leading to strike and other pressure tactics were not tolerated either by the employers or by the society. The working class consciousness emerged with the enactment of Combination Acts in 1979-80 and became stronger during the first half of the nineteenth century. The legality of trade unions was assured under the Trade Unions Act of 1871. But the Criminal Law Amendment Act still considered strike activity as an criminal conspiracy on the ground that it involved coercion. After a gap of thirty years, the Trade Disputes Act of 1906 legalised peaceful persuasion by pickets in connection with disputes. The Trade Disputes and Trade Union Act of 1927 made all picketing at workers' home illegal and restricted pickets even at a work place where a dispute was in progress. The Trade Disputes Act of 1927 was replaced by the Trade Disputes and Trade Union Act of 1946. This Act authorised Government to declare strikes illegal under some conditions. But this order was withdrawn in 1951. The Industrial Relations Act 1971 placed some restrictions on the right to strike.

Under this Act if the National Industrial Relations Court suspected that there was serious risk to the community of the industry it would make an order restraining any step to call, induce, organise or finance industrial actions, including strike and lock-out. During the period the order remained in force, the National Industrial Relations Court could also make an order requiring discontinuance or deterrence of any industrial action including strike.

Such an order of the National Industrial Relations Court can remain in force for sixty days. The Act also authorises the NIRC to impose fines on Unions if they resort to unfair industrial practices.

This Act remained in force for another three years. In 1974 most of the collective provisions of the 1971 Act were repealed.

The effect of this repeal was to restore the law of tort as the only substantial sanction against industrial action (apart from the occasional use of the criminal law particularly against pickets). The Trade Unions and Labour Relations Act 1974 as amended, continued and extended the special protection from the law of tort which had first been granted to industrial activity by the Trade Dispute Act 1906.

In England now the right to strike is an essential element of the principle of collective bargaining. However, the right to strike is not absolute or unconstitutional. It is rationalized in the interest of public safety, health and peace. In fact, in the interest of social good, the right to strike has been restricted in public utility services, public employment and during emergency or war, etc.

RIGHT TO STRIKE IN U.S.A.

The earliest record of a labour disturbance in America goes back to 1635, when a group of fishermen employed by Robert Trelawney at Richmond island went into a "mutiny" when their wages were withheld. Forty years later, when the licensed cartmen of New York were ordered to remove dirt from the streets for three pence a load, they not only protested against the low rate of pay but also "combined in order to refuse full compliance."

The Courts in U.S.A. also adopted the British Common Law Doctrine of Criminal Conspiracy and Restraint of Trade and thus prevented the growth of unionism and also discouraged labour from going on strike.

Persistent struggle of the working class to obtain the right to strike resulted in the enactment of Clayton Act, 1914, which declared that the Federal courts could not restrain employees involved in a labour dispute from engaging in peaceful picketing or boycott carrying out a strike in a peaceful manner and from peacefully assembling in a lawful manner and/or lawful purposes. The struggle did not end there, the working men were not free from court control. The Wagner Act of 1935 and Taft-Hartley Act of 1947 granted employers as well as workers the right to appeal to the National Labour Relations Board against "unfair practices" some of which can be punished by court action. It set new rules for the handling of strikes or disputes which in the judgement of the President of the United States, threatened the national interest. In such cases the President was given the power to appoint a board of enquiry to investigate the situation. A "cooling off" period of eighty days obtained through court injunction would forbid union members to strike during that period. If no suitable agreement was reached within sixty days, a secret pool would be taken among the workers in question as to whether they were willing to accept the last offer made by the employers. After this procedure the injunction must be dissolved even if the dispute has not been settled. Under the law the union is then free to strike.

The Labour-Management Reporting and Disclosure Act of 1959 or popularly known as Landrum-Griffin Act, technically an amendment to Taft-Hartley Act imposed further restrictions on picketing. Consumer picketing is declared to be an unfair labour practice. It also declared that only lawfully recognised unions can picket.

There is no federal law which forbids workers—except government employees to strike. Over the years the government has increasingly concerned itself with the problems of labour disputes and also for safeguarding the national interest. The government reserves the right to intervene in a strike which may affect national interest.

RIGHT TO STRIKE IN INDIA

The labour movement in India, unlike labour movements in other countries, germinated very late. It was only when the First Factory Commission was appointed in 1875, that anything like a working class point of view began to emerge out of the evils associated with the early factory system in India. This germination of the movement was unable to establish itself firmly till the end of the World War I.

The first strike in India took place in 1867. It was by the butchers of Bombay when the corporation decided to shift the slaughter houses to Bandra. Strikes during these periods were quite different from strikes today. In the early strikes, individual workers or groups of workers abandoned their industrial undertakings and migrated to other industrial centres or went back to their villages. There was no attempt at collective bargaining or at obtaining redress through concerted action. Strikes came rather late in India. It was only after 1892 that strikes began to take an organised form. The first such organised strike took place in 1893, when about 8000 workers of cotton textile mills of Bombay participated. However, during this period, workers could not make use of this weapon more often or effectively. It is only after the Ist World War that workers learnt to wage mass struggle over large areas. The end of 1918 saw the first general strike of workers in the cotton mills of Bombay followed by a number of strikes in other industries.

Unlike that of the British Government, the then Indian Government's attitude was not hostile towards workers. It was not because they had any sympathy for industrial workers of India, because it would indirectly serve the interest of the textile manufacturers of Manchester. This is why when textile workers in the Indian mills of Bombay were agitating for reduction in working hours they drew the sympathy of Manchester manufacturers and British manufacturers in India.

The Anglo-Indian Press became the spokesman of Indian labour and expressed its great concern over the disabilities of textile workers. Their efforts led to the enactment of the Factories Act in 1911 which limited the working hours of adult male workers to 12 hours and of children to 6 hours a day. In spite of this sympathy the workers did not enjoy the right to form associations. According to the provisions of the then laws of the land the officers of trade unions were liable to criminal prosecution and also civil action for damages for infringing contractual rights and obligations for interfering with the employers' right to carry on free trade and business.

The general strike of 1918 showed the workers' strength. Employers were concerned over the growing strength of labour. The formation of a national association of workers, the All India Trade Union Congress in 1920, proved beyond any doubt the growing unity and solidarity among industrial workers. Alarmed by this, the employers took the help of the government and also the courts to supress working class movement and prevent them from going on strike. The Buckingham and Carnatic Mills case is a pointer in this direction. When the textile workers of the Mills in Madras went on strike, the employers filed a suit in the Madras High Court asking for damages from Mr. B.P. Wadia and others for instigating workers to go on strike. Relying on the British common law, the Madras High Court granted damages as well as an injunction. Later on when Mr. Wadia agreed to sever his connection with trade union activities, the Mills desisted from recovering the damages from him.

The year 1924 again witnessed a wave of strikes. It was intense in Bombay and Cawnpore. Strike activity was accompanied by violence, which led to firing by troops. The government instituted a case against trade union leaders, which is known as the Cawnpore Conspiracy case or Bolshevik Conspiracy trial, in which four labour leaders were convicted of conspiring to wage war against the King and to spread Bolshevism in India.

The Indian National Congress which was fighting for political freedom of India took up the cause of the working classes and fought for workers' right to form associations. Soon after the decision in the Buckingham and Carnatic Mills case, N.M. Joshi introduced the Trade Union Bill in the Indian Legislature in 1921. The bill was not passed. After five years, in 1926, the first Trade Unions Act became law. It was a landmark in the history of the working class struggle to win the fundamental right of association. The Act provided a legal status to trade unions and immunity to its officers and members from civil and criminal liability for concerted action. A political clause was also provided in the Act to enable the workers to get representation in political bodies.

Since the establishment of All India Trade Union Congress the labour movement in India remained closely associated with the national movement led by the Indian National Congress, which at that time was a strange amalgam of moderates and liberals on the one hand and extremists on the other. Labour unrest increased towards the end of the twenties. The strike record reached its peak in 1928 and was centred in Bombay. By this time the labour movement had fallen into the hands of communists. To curb their influence, the government in 1928 arrested several labour leaders on the charge of criminal conspiracy to overthrow the State. The famous Meerut Trial of 1928 led to their conviction. This proves that even after the enactment of the Trade Unions Act of 1926, courts were being used to protect the interest of industry by bringing charges of criminal offence against trade union leaders.

The year 1929 was another landmark in the workers' struggle for securing normal trade union rights. That year witnessed the enactment of the Trade Disputes Act of 1929, the main purpose of which was to prohibit lightning strikes. The right to strike or lock-out was not recognised in India in earlier days. For the first time it was conceded indirectly under the provisions of the Trade Disputes Act of 1929, which had the main objective of providing a conciliation machinery for peaceful settlement of industrial disputes. Strikes and lock-outs in public utility services without due notice were declared illegal and punishable by law.

During the Second World War, trade union rights were cancelled under the Defence of India Rules. Strikes and lock-outs were prohibited. Provincial governments were empowered to take necessary measures to prevent cessation of work in establishments in which 100 or more persons were engaged. But these emergency powers of the government ceased to be operative from 1946. Independent India witnessed the enactment of the Industrial Disputes Act of 1947 which, among other things, recognised the workers' right to go on strike except in the case of public utility services where a 14 days' notice was required before going on strike.

The Indian Constitution does not consider the right to strike as a fundamental right, and no statute gives the Indian workers the rights that are found in Section 7 and 13 of the National Labour Relations Act in the United States. In the United Kingdom the right to strike is a fundamental right, so long as there is no breach of contract or tort or crime.

Article 19(1) (c) of the Indian Constitution guarantees the citizens the right "to form associations or unions, which is interpreted to include the right to form trade unions. The contention of the trade unions that this right includes the right to engage in concerted activities for mutual aid and protection has, however, been rejected by the courts. In All India Bank Employees' Association Vs. National Industrial Tribunal case, the Supreme Court held that "even a very liberal interpretation of sub clause(c) of cl(1) of Art 19 cannot lead to the conclusion that the trade unions have a guaranteed right to have an effective bargaining or strike. In S. Vasudevan Vs S.D. Metal (1961-62) 21 F.O.R. 441 (H.C. Bombay) case, the High Court held that the right to go on strike is not included in the rights conferred on the citizens under Article 19(1) (c) to form association or unions. Nevertheless, it has been held in another case, Raja Bahadur Motilal Poona Mills Vs Poona Girin

Kamgar Union, 1954 - ILLJ 124 (H.C. Bombay) that employees have a common law right to strike. Chief Justice Chagla observed: "there is nothing inherently unlawful or illegal in a strike .... common law permitted an employee to stop work if he so desired."

This right to strike, however, is not unqualified. It has been held that it should be used only as a last resort when all other avenues have proved futile, and so long as it is used in a restrained, peaceful manner for good and justifiable reasons it cannot be punished. (Caltex Ltd. Vs. Certain Workmen, 1954-LLJ, 516 at 520 (II).

STRIKE AND THE LAW

India

In India the Industrial Disputes Act 1947, is the main instrument of State intervention, which aims at prevention and settlement of disputes through conciliation or compulsory adjudication proceedings or by institution of courts of enquiry. The Act sets forth the circumstances under which strikes and lock-outs are illegal and also provides for advance notice before industrial action can take place.

Under the Industrial Disputes Act, a distinction is made between a strike/lock-out in public utility services and in other employments. Public utility services include the railway service, any section of any establishment on the working of which the safety of the establishment or its workmen depends, the postal, telegraph and telephone service, any industry supplying power, light or water to the public, any system of public conservancy or sanitation, or any of the scheduled industries in respect of which a notification has been issued by the government because of public emergency or public interest.

The Act declares strikes and lock-outs in public utility services to be illegal if they are commenced or declared (a) without giving a notice in the prescribed manner or (b) during the pendency of conciliation proceedings before a conciliation officer and 7 days after the conclusion of such proceedings. All strikes and lock-outs whether in public utility service or not, are deemed to be illegal if they commence or are declared during the pendency of (i) conciliation proceedings before a Board and 7 days after the conclusion of such proceedings, (ii) proceedings before a Tribunal and two months after the conclusion of such proceedings, and (iii) during any period in which a settlement or award is in operation, in respect of any of the matters covered by the settlement or award. Continuance of strike or lock-out is not illegal if it existed prior to the reference of the dispute to a Board or Tribunal provided that such a strike or lock-out is not in contravention of the provisions of the Act when it commenced or its continuance was not prohibited by the Government concerned. A strike or a lock-out declared in consequence of an illegal lock-out by employers or a strike by labourers is not deemed to be illegal. Financial aid in direct furtherance of an illegal strike or lock-out is prohibited under this Act.

A strike or lock-out in contravention of these provisions is illegal and punishable by law.

Under Section 2(g) of the Industrial Disputes Act, 1947, 'strike' means a cessation of work by a body of persons employed in any industry acting in combination or a concerted refusal, or a refusal under common understanding, of any number of persons who are or have been so employed to continue to work or to accept employment.

Ingredients

An industrial strike should have the following ingredients:

(1) Existence of a set of employees and employer maintaining their employment relationships during the period of strikes or lock- outs.

(2) The existence of a dispute (between the strikers and the striken usually but not always e.g., in sympathy strikes or jurisdiction strikes) the settlement of which becomes the object, cause or motive of a strike or lock-out.

(3) Cessation of work by the employees for achieving the object, cause, or propelled by the motive stated in (2) above.

Cessation of Work

This is the most significant characteristic of the concept of strike. It has been variously expressed as 'abandonment' 'stoppage', omission of performance of duties of their posts, 'hampering or reducing normal work', 'hindrance to the working 'suspension of work', discontinuing the employment' or 'breaking their contract of service' or 'refusing or failing to return to resume employment' or 'refusing or failing to accept engagement for any work which they are usually employed.'

The cessation may take any form. It must, however, be temporary and not for ever. No duration can be fixed for this. If the cessation is the result of renunciation of work or relinquishment of the strikers' status or relationship, it is not strike.

The cessation must be of work; it may be nominal as in token strikes for a few minutes only or it may be within the walls of the establishment as in the case of sit-down and stay-in-strikes with the workers remaining in their seats. Though the cessation of work is generally simultaneous and collective, yet it is not necessary. Mass casual leave and refusal to resume work is also strike. In all countries the strike involves a cessation of work, but it is a collective action and does not represent a decision on the part of workers to leave the organisation permanently.

In addition to the statutory measures adopted by the Government of India for the prevention of strikes and the settlement of industrial disputes, some industrially advanced States have enacted special Acts to meet their individual requirements. The lead in this respect was taken by the Government of Bombay.

Under the Bombay Industrial Relations Act of 1946, approved unions and employers are authorised to appear before a labour court in a proceeding for determining whether a strike/lock-out is illegal.

The Act provides that approved unions staging or instigating an illegal strike shall not be entitled to registration. According to the Act, strikes should not be undertaken until all methods under the Act have been exhausted and the majority of the members vote in favour of strike.

The Uttar Pradesh Industrial Disputes Act 1947 is a simple enactment giving the state government power to prohibit strikes and lock-outs, to refer industrial disputes for conciliation or adjudication, to enforce adjudication awards on the parties to the dispute and to exercise control over and public utility service. The

Act was amended in 1950 and 1953. This Act empowered the Government to prevent strikes and lock-outs. Section 3 of the State Act gives an elaboration of the powers given to the government to fulfil the objective of preventing strikes and lock-outs.

This section provides that, if in the opinion of the State Government it is necessary or expedient so to do for securing public safety or convenience or the maintenance of public order or supplies and services essential to the life of the community or for maintaining employment, it may by a general or a special order, make provisions :—(a) for prohibiting, subject to the provisions of the order, strikes or lock-outs generally; or (b) strikes or lock-outs in connection with any particular industrial dispute.

The Essential Services Maintenance Act 1968 empowers Government to ban strikes in Essential Services, and to declare prohibited strikes to be illegal, and provides penalties to persons instigating and financing such strikes. Under section 2(1)a of the Act, Essential Services mean :

(i) any postal, telephone or telegraph service,

(ii) any railway service or any other transport service for the carriage of passengers or goods by land, water or air,

(iii) any service connected with the operation, repair or maintenance of aircraft,

(iv) any service connected with the loading or unloading, movement or storage of goods in any part,

(v) any service connected with the clearance of goods or passengers through the customs or with the prevention of smuggling,

(vi) any service in any security press,

(vii) any service in any defence establishment of the Government of India,

(viii) any service in connection with the affairs of the Union of India, not being a service specified in any of the fore-going sub- clauses,

(ix) and other services connected with matters with respect to which Parliament has power to make laws and

> which the Central Government being of opinion that strikes therein would prejudicially affect the maintenance of any public utility service, the public safety or the maintenance of supplies and services necessary for the life of the community or would result in the infliction of grave hardships on the community, may be notification in the official gazette, declare to be an essential service for the purpose of this Act.

The prohibitions which make a strike illegal in India are merely procedural in nature. The object of the strike is not the issue. It would not be illegal or unlawful to strike in public utilities provided a proper notice is served on the employers. The procedural prohibitions on strikes in India are quite close to the restrictions prescribed in Sections 8(d) of the Labour Management Relations Act of U.S.A.. In both India and the United States advance notices must be served, and certain specified acts performed. But in Indian law there is no counterpart of Section 8(b) or Section 303 of the Labour Management Relations Act which makes a strike illegal because of unlawful objectives. If a strike is found to be in violation of Section 8(b) or Section 303(a) of the Labour Management Relations Act, the strikers lose the protection of the Act. In India a mere participation in an illegal strike does not terminate a worker's relationship with his employer. The employer is not free to discharge the striker, unless there is such a standing order of the company. The employer is, however, free to force a lock-out if the strike is illegal, and the workers cannot recover wages for the lock-out period.

The only punishment which the law prescribes is criminal prosecution where-by an employee may receive a maximum punishment of one month's imprisonment and a fine of Rs. 50/- and the instigators and financiers of the strike a maximum punishment of six months imprisonment and a fine of Rs. 1000/-.

Injunctions against strikes in India cannot be secured by the employer or by an industrial administrative agency. Strikes can be prohibited by the appropriate Federal or State Government through an executive order, and only when the dispute is referred to an industrial tribunal for adjudication.

Commencing on the statutory provisions relating to strikes, the National Commission on Labour, stated that labour has devised new forms of agitation such as go-slow, work-to-rule, etc. which fall beyond the purview of statutory provisions relating to strikes. The Commission has suggested suitable widening of the definition of strike to include all such forms of agitation. They are of opinion that legal restrictions alone cannot help in reducing strikes and other forms of labour unrest, unless the Government find it expedient to do so in several cases, a mere classification of concerted action on the part of workers/employers as illegal will only bring the law into disrepute.

In 1978, the Janata Government proposed in the Industrial Relations Bill that every decision to go on a strike shall be supported by not less than sixty per cent of the employees in a strike ballot conducted under the general supervision and superintendence of the Registrar of the Trade Unions. The Registrar will also have the power to decide any dispute pertaining to a strike ballot, the dispute being raised either by an employee or an employer. A strike section with such a support will acquire a certain degree of legitimacy and will, therefore, not be called irresponsible.

Commenting on the Industrial Relations Bill, 1978, Dr. G.P. Sinha said in his presidential address of the 21st annual conference of the Indian Society of Labour Economics, (Oct. 12- 14, 1979) that to demand a strike decision be supported by a minimum of sixty per cent of employees in a secret ballot conducted by the Registrar, is based on wrong assumptions. One of the assumptions is that the workers are, by and large, less militant and much more in a better position to appraise the implications of the issues which necessitate a strike and the trade union leaders are the villains of the peace. Anyone who has a nodding acquaintance with the working of the trade unions will find that unless the leaders are pressurised by the workers for action they cannot foist a strike decision on them. This is the situation in an overwhelming number of cases and so, it would never be difficult for any leader to secure sixty per cent support. Therefore, such a provision would be an unnecessary irritant and uncalled for interference by the government in the domestic affairs of the unions.

This Industrial Relations Bill was introduced in Lok Sabha in August 1978, but as the Parliament was dissolved it could not be considered and so lapsed.

THE TRADE UNIONS AND THE INDUSTRIAL DISPUTES (AMENDMENT) BILL, 1988

The Trade Unions and the Industrial Disputes (Amendment) Bill 1988 is supposed to be based on the recommendations of the National Commission on Labour (1969). The recommendations of the Commission were considered by the National Conference on Labour in September 1982. On the unanimous recommendation of the conference a committee was set up to examine the specific issues referred to it. The considered recommendations of the committee were discussed by the Standing Labour Committee in September 1986.

On the basis of the recommendations of the above committees, it was considered necessary to undertake comprehensive amendments to the Trade Union Act, 1926 and the Industrial Dispute Act 1947. The declared objectives of the Bill are:

(1) To set up statutory frame-work, institutions for promoting peace and harmony in industry;

(2) To protect the legitimate interest of workers and employers for increased production and productivity, increased flow of goods and services;

(3) Consequent improvement in the standard of living of the people;

(4) A greater measure of social justice;

(5) Promote responsible internally led trade unions which can be engaged in collective bargaining with employer with a full sense of the confidence reposed in them by substantial sections of the workers and

(6) Which gives both workers and employers a stake in jointly searching for settlements and evolving mutually beneficial collective bargaining forums without recourse to competing militancy among non-representative or fragmented trade unions or unnecessary or prolonged litigation.

It is proposed to set up Industrial Relations Commissions both at the Centre and States. These will comprise both judicial and non-judicial members. The non-judicial members will be drawn from among persons having experience in the fields of industry, labour or management. The IRC will be high powered tribunals under article 323 (B) of the Constitution and appeals against their orders or awards will be made only to the Supreme Court of India.

The Bill seeks to provide that for a Union to be registered it must have a membership of at least 10 per cent of the total workforce in an establishment where the number of such workmen is one hundred or more. For smaller establishments the minimum requirements of seven members will continue.

The proposed Bill provides for not more than two non-employees as office bearers from non-workers. The Bill also puts a limit to seven number of Trade Unions, on which an individual can hold office. The Bill provides check-off system for verification of membership. Under check-off system each worker will give the management in writing the name of the Union he or she belongs to and authorise it to deduct union fees from wages. The check-off system would be normally adopted for verification of membership though there is provision for the holding of secret ballot in certain exceptional circumstances.

The Bill provides for the constitution of a bargaining council for a three-year term to negotiate and settle industrial disputes with the employer. While the Unit-level bargaining council will be set up by the employer the appropriate Government will be empowered to set up such council at industry level. All the registered unions will be represented on the bargaining council in proportion to their relative strength but any union with a strength of not less than 40 per cent of the total membership of the workmen in an industrial establishment will be recognised, as the 'Principal bargaining agent'. In the absence of a registered trade union in an establishment, the Bill envisages setting up of workmen's council for collective bargaining.

All bargaining councils are to be registered by the Labour Court and under certain circumstances its registration may be cancelled. The bargaining council can raise a dispute, settle a dispute, sign an agreement, represent the workers in any industrial dispute and can exercise such other powers as may be prescribed.

The Bill makes a specific provision for bipartite negotiations. The Bill also lays stress on the need to exhaust all modes of settlement like bipartite discussions, conciliation, voluntary arbitration, etc., before resort to direct action. Even for the last resort i.e. strike or lock-out the conditions prescribed must be met by either party contemplating it with corresponding penalties for resorting to such extreme steps in contravention of the law.

The Bill provides for direct reference to industrial disputes (including disputes arising out of discharge, dismissal, retrenchment or termination of service due to any reason) to a Labour Court for adjudication by the concerned workman or by trade union in case conciliation fails.

The Bill provides that failure to pay legitimate dues to the workmen concerned by the employer at the time of closure or retrenchment would entail compulsory imprisonment and also a fine of an amount equal to the amount of such unpaid compensation and wages which shall not be less than Rs. 5000/-. Besides, an application for retrenchment/closer by an employer will be considered only when he undertakes to discharge the liability for all dues of the workmen concerned or when the application is supported by an irrevocable bank guarantee.

The amending Bill provides for compulsory election of office bearers of Trade Unions every year.

The Bill proposes that a collective agreement reached by the bargaining council or bargaining agent will bind only parties to the agreement.

On the whole the Bill aims at setting up of a statutory framework within which strikes and lock-outs are substantially reduced. Further workers are likely to get justice in spite of indifference of the management and unions. There are likely to be less number of trade unions and unions, involvement in political activities is likely to be restricted.

Strike being an important aspect of labour-management relations have attracted the attention of sociologists, psychologists, economists, legislators and all other persons who deal with such relations. Some of the authors have analysed strike with an international perspective and have tried to explain the causes for variations in the pattern and nature of strikes. Others have explained strike activity keeping only the national perspective in view. Again most of these studies are based on conditions existing in developed countries where the situation is very different from that prevailing in developing or developed countries. Hence, difficulty arises in applying these concepts in developing and under developed countries.

Among the studies on strikes with an international perspective, mention may be made of Kerr and Siegel, Ross and Hartman and others. Both Ross and Hartman and Kerr–Siegel have agreed that strikes are withering away, but differ on the courses of the withering process. Kerr and Siegel attribute such withering to the workers integration in the wider society, whereas Ross and Hartman attribute it to economic reasons.

Kerr-Siegel thesis has been rejected by Kuhn, Knowles and others. Kuhn's emphasis on technology as an important factor has been discussed by Goldthorpe. He argues that the orientations which the workers have towards their employment is more important than either technology or formal organisations. Strike frequency, according to Knowles increases when employment and profits rise. The tendency for increase in strike frequency when profits and employment are rising, stems from the feeling that the prospects of extracting concessions are better and possible penalties of failure seem less. Besides Knowles, several other authors have made studies of strikes vis-a-vis business cycles. Sheila V. Hopkins, Weintraule, John Shorey, Albert Rees and others have said that business cycles exert profound influence on industrial unrest.

The findings of Knowles, Sheila, Rees and others that strike activity increases during prosperity have been rejected by Theodore Levitt. Levitt has argued that the economic staying capacity of workers weakens during prosperity and this makes unions less capable of sustaining a strike.

Edward Shorter and Charles Tilly have found that intimate relations exist between industrial structure, organisational base of working class life and workers' participation in politics and strike activity. Making an international comparison the authors show how different patterns of workers involvement in politics have led, especially since the Second World War, to differences in the structure of strike from one country to another.

Studies on strikes in India are made by V.B. Karnik, Ishwar Dayal and B.R. Sharma, Pandey and Pathak, P. Prakash Arya, Konda Reddy, etc. The studies discussed above emphasised on four factors economic, organisational, political and psychological for the occurence of strikes. Most of the studies stress the importance of economic determinants like changes in real wages and business cycles and have statistically proved that strike activity increases during prosperity and declines at the time of depression. Employment opportunities, ratio of profits to wages, cost of price index, wage rate changes are the four major variables on which most of the studies are concentrated. However, the institutional political and psychological factors cannot be ignored, rather, these factors have become more significant in developed countries.

2

STRIKES IN ORISSA: A WIDER SETTING

Strike activity being the result of various factors, this chapter begins with a brief discussion of the industrial environment of Orissa for a better understanding of the problem as it relates to this State.

In Orissa industrial development started very late resulting in a late start of the trade union movement too. The workers of small industrial organisations like rice mills, printing presses, etc. were unable to use strike as a weapon against their employer, for offensive and defensive purposes. Strike activity, therefore, was not marked during forties and fifties of the present century.

Industrialization in Orissa began with the Second Five Year Plan (1956-60) when emphasis was placed on rapid development of industries. The commencement of the Hirakud Dam Project gave fillip to industrialization and a number of new units emerged both in private and public sectors—like. The Indian Aluminium Company Limited (INDAL), 1958, The Rourkela Steel Plant (RSP), 1960, The Jayakaypur Paper Mills (J.K. Paper Mills), 1960 etc. giving rise to an increase in the number of factories and industrial employment. The number of factories increased from 384 in 1958 to 424 in 1970 i.e. an increase of 150.5 per cent. Industrial employment also increased by 14 per cent during the fifties and by 15 per cent during the sixties.

Industrialization gave birth to unionisation. Though Orissa saw the birth of first trade union only in 1935, when workers of the Rambha Rice Mill formed their union, unionism in fact started during the fifties. In 1937 only one union was functioning with 18 members, which increased to 84 with 26,206 members in 1950. The table given below shows the growth of trade unions in Orissa since 1950.

Table 2.1. Growth of trade unions in Orissa since 1950

Year	*No. of Trade Unions*	*Index*	*Union Membership*	*Index*
1950	84	100	26,206	100
1960	107	127	58,157	222
1970	216	257	1,11,799	427
1980	671	799	3,21,411	1226
1987	892	1062	5,80,069	2213

Source: The Labour Directorate, Government of Orissa.

In 1950, 84 unions with 26,206 members existed. The number of unions increased to 107 and membership rose to 58,157 in 1960. In 1970, the number of unions increased more than two and half time and the membership more than twice the number. But in 1980, the number of unions increased nearly 8 times and membership more than 12 times. In 1987, the number of unions increased by more than ten and half times and membership by twenty-two times. This shows that over the decades trade unions have acquired numerical strength and stabilized their position. This strong base of unionisation inspired the workers to use strike as a weapon against their employers to force their demands.

With this background it is proposed to examine and analyse strike activity during 1960's and 1980's. This chapter intends to provide a wider perspective to the ensuing examination of strike activity in Orissa.

The Trends of Industrial Disputes and Work-Stoppages

To study the general trend of industrial disputes and work-stoppages during the sixties and seventies, data on frequency of disputes and work-stoppages, number of man-days lost, workers involved, are analysed. The table 2.2 shows the index number of industrial disputes and work-stoppages in Orissa between 1960 and 1989.

Table 2.2.Trend of industrial disputes and work- stoppages during 1961-89

Period	*No. of industrial dispute*	*Index of industrial dispute*	*No. of work-stoppages*	*Index of work-stoppages*
1961-65	907	100	104	100
1966-70	1703	187	138	133
1971-75	2065	227	216	208
1976-80	2672	294	424	408
1981-85	3927	433	411	395
1986-89	4329	477	323	310

Source: i) The Labour Directorate, Government of Orissa.
.Work-stoppages include both strikes and lock-outs.
1989 statistics on work-stoppages provisional.

The analysis shows that both the industrial disputes and work-stoppages increased over the period under study. The number of industrial disputes which was 907 during the first part of 1960's increased to 4329, during the last part of 1980's. The number of work-stoppages also increased from 104 during 1961-65 to 323 during 1986-89. Over a period of three decades, industrial disputes increased by more than four and half times and work - stoppages by more than three times. The index number of industrial disputes increased from 100 during 1961-65 to 477 during 1986-89 and that of work-stoppages to 310. From 1976 onwards data on work-stoppages do not show continuous increasing trend. With year to year variations, periodic decreasing trend is noticed between 1976-89.

Further analysis shows that the proportion of work-stoppages to industrial disputes also increased. During 1960's, out of every 100 disputes, on an average 9 disputes resulted in work- stoppages but the proportion increased to 14 during 1970's. Between 1981-89, it is 8.8. The table given below shows the proportion of work-stoppages to disputes.

Table 2.3. Proportion of work-stoppages to industrial disputes

Period	*No. of industrial disputes*	*No. of work-stoppages*	*Percentage of work-stoppages to industrial disputes*
1960's	2610	242	9.2
1970's	4737	640	13.5
1980's	8256	734	8.8

Source: The Labour Directorate, Government of Orissa.

The analysis thus shows that with an increase in factory employment and unionisation—both industrial disputes and work-stoppages have increased. But work-stoppages have increased at a rate faster than that of industrial disputes during 1970's. Between 1981-89, there is low decrease in the proportion work- stoppages to industrial disputes. However, the state conciliation machinery is playing an effective role in the settlement of disputes and in controlling strike activity. Even if the workers resort to strike, conciliation machinery intervenes to restore normalcy and is successful in almost 60 per cent of the cases.

DISTRIBUTION OF WORK-STOPPAGES BETWEEN STRIKES AND LOCK-OUTS

The table given below shows the distribution of work- stoppages between strikes and lock-outs.

Table 2.4. Percentage distribution of strikes and lock-outs

Period	*No. of strikes*	*No. of lock-outs*	*Percentage of strikes*	*Percentage of lock-outs*
1960's	229	13	94.7	5.3
1970's	603	37	94.3	5.7
1980's	658	76	89.6	11.4

Source: The Labour Directorate, Government of Orissa.

The above table shows that during the 1960's, 94.7 per cent of work-stoppages were due to strikes and only 5.3 per cent due to lock-outs. But during 1970's strikes accounted for 94.3 per cent and lock-outs 5.7 per cent, registering an increase of about 0.2 per cent during the seventies. Between 1981-89 lock-outs accounted for 11.4 per cent which shows that within a period of nine years it increased by 5.7 per cent.

The possible explanation for the low percentage of lock-outs in comparison to strikes may be the fact that the employers mostly declare lock-outs if the strike action goes out of control. In Orissa, it is learnt from the official sources that almost all the lock-outs were declared in response to strikes. The second possible explanation may be the fact that when the employer declares a lock-out, he has to bear the entire loss of production. If there were any chances of circumventing the provisions of the law, the workers would not hesitate to declare a strike. So the employer has to give a second thought when he decides to declare a lock-out.

The statistical analysis also reveals that in India during the 1960's only 8 per cent of the work-stoppages were recorded as being due to lock-outs and 92 per cent due to strikes. But during the 1970's, lock-outs accounted for 12 per cent and strikes registered 88 per cent only. Man-days lost due to lock-out were 28 per cent during the 1960's and 35 per cent during the 1970's. Thus we find that in Orissa as in India as a whole work-stoppages due to lock-outs have been gradually increasing. During 1980's out of 100 work-stoppages eleven are lock-outs, whereas it was only 5 during 1970's.

TRENDS IN FREQUENCY OF STRIKES, WORKERS' INVOLVEMENT AND MAN-DAYS LOST

All the three measures of strike activity, viz. strike frequency, worker involvement, and man-days lost are analysed to examine the movement of strikes between 1961 and 1989. The number of strikes shows the frequency of conflict, participation ratio, and loss due to strikes demonstrate the magnitude of the problem. The table 2.5 shows the number and index number of strikes, workers involvement, and man-days lost.

The table shows that all the three variables viz. frequency of strikes, workers involvement, and man-days lost show an increasing trend. The number of strikes increased from 103 during 1961-65 to 393 during 1976-80. Between 1981-85, the frequency of strikes increased by more than three and half times worker involvement by more than four times and man-days lost by nearly three times.

Table 2.5. Trend in Strike Measures from 1961 to 1989

Period	*No. of strikes*		*Workers involved*		*Man-days Lost*	
	No.	*Index*	*No.*	*Index*	*No.*	*Index*
1961-65	103	100	40014	100	2822765	100
1966-70	126	122	39392	098	440394	156
1971-75	210	204	66918	167	746985	265
1976-80	393	382	104477	261	789901	277
1981-85	371	360	165674	414	1058521	374
1986-89	286	278	149296	373	1169352	413

Source: The Labour Directorate, Government of Orissa, 1989 data provisional.

Between 1986-89, the number of strikes increased by roughly three times and worker involvement by more than three and half times. During the period 1961-80 the number of workers involved increased from 40014 to 104477 and man-days lost from 282765 to 789901. The index number of strike frequency has increased nearly four times, worker involvement more than two and half times and man-days lost nearly three times over the two decades i.e. the 1960's and the 1970's. All these data thus provide a clear indication of increasing trend of strike activity in Orissa between 1960-80. The incidence strikes both in absolute numbers and relative to the labour force available for participation in conflict rose from 1961 to 1980 steadily which fluctuated at a low level between 1981-85, e.g., as it was shown in table 2.5 the index of strikes in absolute number increased from 100 between 1961-65 to 382 between 1976-80 which decreased to 360 between 1981-85. Strikes per thousand employees which was 0.306 during 1960's rose to 0.749 during the seventies which came down to 0.486 during the 1980's. It might be due to incomplete data for the period of one decade man-days lost per employee also shows a fluctuated trend as it increased by 0.5 between 1960's and 1980's but when compared between 1970's and 1980's it decreased by 0.4 days. Average size of strike shows a fluctuated decreasing trend during the period of analysis because on an average roughly 478 workers participated in a strike during 1960's which decreased to 451 during 1980's. During 1970's only

290 workers participated in a strike. But the length of strike decreased almost steadily from 1960's to 1980's.

The unionisation progressed steadily from 1950 onwards. The number of trade unions increased by ten and half times and membership by more than 22 times. Each of the principal increase in strike activity was tied to an increase in the organization capacity of labour.

The decrease both in number and membership of trade unions in 1986 resulted in reduction of strike activity during the period 1986-89. Between 1985 and 1986 there was reduction of roughly twelve per cent in number of trade unions and more than seven per cent in membership. In 1985 the number of trade unions were 919 with 6,10,500 membership which reduced to 810 and 5,65,660 respectively in 1986.

The present analysis of strike activity between 1960's and 1980's does not confirm any continuous periodic trend because of year to year variations in strike frequency, size loss due to strikes.

But between 1960's and 1970's there was a clear indication of continuous increasing trend.

An analysis of the rate of growth of the above mentioned three measures of strike activity reveals another interesting feature that workers involvement and man-days lost are increasing at a very high rate. But the average duration and average size of strike show decreasing trend. To measure the rate of growth, the method of Least Square is used. The following equations are solved to measure the value of 'b' which stands for the rate of growth of strike measures from 1961 to 1980 and from 1981-89.

$Y = na + bx$

$xy = ax + bx^2$

y is dependent variable (which stands for number of strikes/ workers involved/man-days lost)

x is independent variable (years)

Measuring by the method, we arrive at the following results:

	Rate of growth	
	1961-80	1981-89
Number of strikes	3.81	– 0.95
Workers involved	906.81	1004.23
Man-days lost	7649.56	26485.86
Strikes per-thousand employees	0.04	–0.001
Man-days lost per striker	0.21	0.857
Strikes per strike	29.12	15.45

The result thus shows that the highest rate of growth has been in the area of man-days lost. The rate of growth is much higher between 1981-89 in comparison to 1961-80. The rate of growth is lowest in the case of strike frequency between 1961-80 and it is negative during 1981-89. The rate of growth of workers' involvement is also pretty high but not in the same proportion as the man-days lost. It is also higher during the period 1981-89 when compared with the period 1961-80. The average size of strike has been reduced during 1981-89 when compared with the period 1961-80 whereas the growth rate of average duration has been increased by more than four times.

The analysis of secondary measures like strikes per thousand employees, man-days lost per employee, etc. also shows the increasing trend of strike activity with periodic activity in Orissa. For example, strike per thousand employees which was 0.306 during the sixties rose to 0.749 during the seventies and 0.486 during the 1980's. But the average duration (man-days lost per striker) decreased from 11.321 days to 10.151 days during the period under study. The table given below shows the trend of secondary measures of strike activity during the 1960's and the 1980's.

Again, when worker involvement in strike activity is compared with the volume of industrial employment, it appears that their involvement during the period has increased considerably. During the sixties, roughly 13 per cent of industrial labour force was involved in strike activity which increased to roughly 23 per cent

Table 2.6. Trend of secondary measures of strike activity during the 1960's and the 1980's

Period	*Strike per thousand employees (Frequency of strike)*	*Workers involved per strike (Average size of a strike)*	*Man-days lost per worker involved (Average duration)*	*Man-days lost per employee (loss due to strike)*
1960's	0.306	477.700	11.321	1.17
1970's	0.749	289.286	11.193	1.96
1980's	0.486	450.922	10.151	1.58

during the seventies and to more than 26 per cent during 1980's. The table 2.7 shows the percentage of worker involvement in strikes in relation to the total industrial employment during the 1960's and the 1980's.

Table 2.7. Percentage of worker involvement in strike activity to industrial employment during 1960's and 1980's

Period	*Employment* (in lakhs)*	*Workers[1] involvement (in lakhs)*	*Percentage[2]*
1960's	6.07	0.79	13.01
1970's	7.83	1.71	22.90
1980's	11.25	2.97	26.40

Source: *Statistical Abstract of Orissa, Bureau of Statistics.
[1]Labour Directorate, Government of Orissa.
[2]Economic Survey of Orissa - 1990, Annexure No. 7.1.

MAN-DAYS LOST PER STRIKE

It has been mentioned in table 2.8 that among the three measures of strike activity, the average rate of growth was highest in the area to aggregate man-days lost. But when man-days lost are compared in terms of each strike, it is observed that man-days lost per strike declined during the seventies. The index number declined from 100 during the sixties to 61 during the seventies. This shows that even though the strike activity has increased but not worker's militancy. Necessary data showing man-days lost per strike during the 1960's and the 1980's are given in the following table.

Table 2.8. Loss of man-days per strike during the 1960's and the 1970's

Period	*Loss of man-days per strike*	*Index of man-days lost*
1960's	4084.50	100
1970's	2849.97	61
1980's	3437.24	84

Source: The Labour Directorate, Government of Orissa.

TREND IN STRIKE ACTIVITY IN ORISSA AND INDIA (AS A WHOLE)

A comparison of strike data of Orissa with those of the country as a whole would show that strike frequency in India during 1970's increased by 32 per cent, worker involvement by 69 per cent and man-days lost by 139 per cent. During 1980's, the strike frequency decreased by 21 per cent, worker involvement increased by 8 per cent and man-days lost by 85 per cent. As against this, in Orissa, strike frequency increased by 163 per cent, worker involvement by 116 per cent and man-days lost by 113 per cent. During 1980's strike frequency increased by 187 per cent, worker involvement by 297 per cent and man-days lost by 208 per cent. This shows that in comparison to India as a whole, frequency of strike and worker involvement in Orissa increased at a higher rate. The comparative figures are given in the following table.

Table 2.9. Trend of strike frequency, worker involvement and man- days loss in India (as a whole) and Orissa

Strike	*India (as a whole)*			*Orissa*		
Measure	*1960s*	*1970s*	*1980s*	*1960s*	*1970s*	*1980s*
No. of strikes	20662	27369	16244	229	603	657
Index of strikes	100	132	79	100	263	287
No. of workers involved	11156983	18867853	12057000	79406	171395	314970

Index of workers involved	100	169	108	100	216	397
No. of man-days lost (000)	102297	244347	291312	723159	1536886	2227873
Index of man-days lost	100	239	285	100	213	308

Source: (i) Labour Bureau, Ministry of Labour, Government of India.
(ii) Labour Directorate, Government of Orissa.

STRIKES IN MANUFACTURING AND NON-MANUFACTURING SECTORS

A study of strikes in manufacturing and non-manufacturing sectors reveals that strike activity is concentrated mainly in the manufacturing sector. On an average, 90 per cent of strikes occurred in the manufacturing sector and only 10 per cent in the non-manufacturing sector during the 1960's. Again, the manufacturing sector accounted for 96 per cent of man-days lost. But during the 1970s, the share of the non-manufacturing sector registered a small rise in strike frequency. Almost 79 per cent of strikes occurred in the manufacturing sector. During 1980's the non-manufacturing sector share is 15 per cent of man-days lost. The table given below shows the percentage distribution of strikes and man-days lost in the manufacturing and non- manufacturing sectors.

Table 2.10. Percentage distribution of strikes and man-days lost in the manufacturing and non-manufacturing sectors during 1960's and 1970's

Name of the Industrial sector	*1960's*		*1970's*		*1980's*	
	No. of Strikes	*Man-days Lost*	*No. of Strikes*	*Man-days Lost*	*No. of Strikes*	*Man-days Lost*
Manufacturing sector	90	96	79	94	90	85
Non-manufacturing sector	10	04	21	06	10	15

Source: Labour Directorate, Government of Orissa.

Three possible reasons may be given for this high degree of difference between the manufacturing sector and the non-manufacturing sector. Firstly, about 63 per cent of workers are employed in the manufacturing sector and 37 per cent in the non-manufacturing sector covered in this study. The table 2.11 shows the percentage distribution of workers employed in the manufacturing and non-manufacturing sectors.

Secondly, on an average a trade union in the manufacturing sector has 901 members, whereas a union in the non-manufacturing sector has only 251.

Table 2.11. Distribution of workers between manufacturing and non-manufacturing sector

Year	*No. of Factories Operating*	*Total No. of Workers*	*No. of Workers*		*Percentage*	
			Manufacturing	*Non-Manufacturing*	*Manufacturing*	*Non-Manufacturing*
1974-75	809	76,064	47,868	28,196	62.9	37.1
1975-76	819	82,276	49,582	32,694	60.2	39.8
1976-77	872	83,826	50,621	33,205	60.3	39.7
1977-78	957	86,381	53,902	32,479	62.4	37.6
1978-79	1006	86,431	59,602	26,829	68.9	31.1
1979-80	1171	97,307	61,552	35,755	63.2	36.8
Total		5,12,285	3,23,027	1,89,158	63.05	36.9

Source: 1. Compiled from the Statistical Abstract of Orissa, Bureau of Statistics and Economics, Government of Orissa, 1979, p. 99, 1981, p. 294.
2. Economic Survey of Orissa, Annexure No. 7.8

Table 2.12 shows the average size of the unions in the manufacturing and non-manufacturing sectors.

Thirdly, the manufacturing sector is better unionised than the non-manufacturing sector. In 1961 the degree of unionisation in the manufacturing sector was 32 per cent, whereas it was 0.61 per cent in the non-manufacturing sector. But over the years the degree of unionisation has increased considerably both in the manufacturing

Table 2.12. Average membership per union in manufacturing and non-manufacturing sectors

Year	*Unions*		*Membership*		*Membership per union*	
	Manu-facturing Indus-tries	*Non-Manu-facturing Indus-tries*	*Manu-facuring Indus-tries*	*Non-Manu-facturing Indus-tries*	*Manu-factur-ing Indus-tries*	*Non-Manu-facturing Indus-tries*
1978	258	277	1,64,325	87,121	637	593
1979	288	310	1,81,983	97,931	632	316
1980	325	346	2,13,517	1,07,899	557	312
1981	359	379	2,42,914	1,25,865	677	332
1982	353	365	2,49,516	1,28,935	707	353
1983	386	408	2,53,470	1,30,980	657	321
1984	415	436	3,21,371	2,24,531	774	515
1985	445	474	3,50,282	2,60,318	787	449
1986	402	408	3,26,087	2,39,573	811	587
1987	411	451	3,34,322	2,36,717	813	525
Total	3642	3854	26,38,087	16,39,870	724	425

Source: Annual list of Trade Unions, 1978 to 1987, Labour Directorate, Orissa, Bhubaneswar, Book-Trade Unions and Politics in India; P.C. Das, p. 45.

and the non-manufacturing sectors. But the improvement was more marked in the manufacturing sector. In the manufacturing sector, the degree of unionisation increased to 47.8 per cent in 1971, whereas it was only 3.2 per cent in the non-manufacturing sector. Details of unionism in manufacturing and non-manufacturing sectors are given in the table below.

Table 2.13. Degree of unionisation in manufacturing and non-manufacturing sectors

Name of the industrial sector	*Degree of unionisation 1961*	*Degree of unionisation 1971*
Manufacturing sector	32.25	47.8
Non-manufacturing sector	0.61	3.2

Source: The Labour Directorate, Government of Orrissa.

The impact of unionisation and employment might be the contributing factor of increased strike activity in the manufacturing sector rather than in the non-manufacturing sector.

STRIKES IN PUBLIC AND PRIVATE SECTORS

The table below gives the index number of strike frequency in public and private sectors during 1960-89.

Table 2.14. Distribution of strikes in public and private sectors

Period	*Public sector*		*Private sector*	
	No. of strikes	*Index No. of strikes*	*No. of strikes*	*Index No. of strikes*
1966-70	40	100	86	100
1971-75	96	240	114	133
1976-80	128	320	265	308
1981-85	123	308	248	288
1986-89	81	203	193	224

Source: Labour Directorate, Government of Orissa.

It appears from the above table that between 1966-70 and 1971-75, strike activity increased at a faster rate in the public sector undertaking. The index number increased from 100 to 240 in the public sector and to 133 in the private sector. But during the second half of the seventies i.e. 1976-80, the private sector witnessed a sharp increase in strike activity. The index number increased from 133 to 308. But in the public sector, the increase was not so sharp. It increased from 240 to 320. But on the whole between 1966-70 and 1971-80, the public sector witnessed a faster rate of growth in strike activity than the private sector. During 1981-85, the public sector also shows a faster rate of growth than the private sector as the index number in case of public sector is 308 and in private sector it is 288. But between 1986-89 the index number is 203 in public sector and 224 in private sector. But on the whole between 1981-89 in both the sectors the number of strikes increased by more than 5 times.

In spite of this rising trend of both the number of strikes and man-days lost in the public sector undertakings, strikes are still concentrated largely in the private sector. Between 1966-70, roughly 72 per cent of strikes occurred in the private sector and 84 per cent of man-days lost should be accounted for in this sector. During this period the public sector accounted for only 28 per cent of strikes and 16 per cent of the man-days lost. Between 1981-89 the public sector witnessed 32 per cent of strikes and 34 per cent of man-days lost. The table below gives the percentage distribution of strikes and man-days lost in public and private sector undertakings.

Table 2.15. Percentage distribution of strikes and man-days lost in public and private sector undertakings

Period	*Public Sector*		*Private Sector*	
	No. of strikes	*Man-days lost*	*No. of strikes*	*Man-days lost*
1966-70	32	06	68	94
1971-80	37	21	63	79
1981-89	32	34	68	66

Source: Labour Directorate, Government of Orissa.

The rising trend of strike activity between 1971-80 in the public sector may be attributed to the fact that more and more industrial units have come up in this sectors. It has also registered a positive growth rate in number of unions. The growth rate over a decade shows that the number of unions has increased at a faster rate in the public sector than in the private sector. The table given below shows the number of trade unions and the index number during the 1960's and the 1980's.

Table 2.16. Distribution of unions between public and private sectors

Period	*Public Sector*		*Private Sector*	
	No. of unions	*Index No. of unions*	*No. of unions*	*Index No. of unions*
1966-70	0453	100	0594	100
1971-80	1838	405	1850	311
1981-87	3281	724	2441	411

Source: Labour Directorate, Government of Orissa.

In the public sector the number of unions increased from 453 in 1966-70 to 1838 in 1971-80 which became almost doubled between 1981-87. In the private sector it increased from 594 to 1850 during 1971-80 and it increased to 2441 between 1981-87. In both the sectors a positive growth rate is registered. The unions have increased more than 4 times in the public sector and roughly 3 times in the private sector. Between 1966-70 it increased by more than 7 times in public sector and by more than 4 times in private sector. Union membership also registered a positive growth rate in both the sectors but the public sector recorded a higher growth rate in comparison with the private sector. The growth rate of union membership in the public and the private sectors is given in the following table.

Table 2.17. Index of union members in public and private sectors

Period	*Public Sector*		*Private Sector*	
	No. of Union Members	*Index of Union Members*	*No. of Union Members*	*Index of Union Members*
1966-70	278359	100	302611	100
1971-80	1044307	375	723697	239
1981-87	2221660	798	1212151	401

Source: Labour Directorate, Government of Orissa.

Union membership increased more than 3 and half times in the public sector during 1966-80. But the private sector witnessed an increase to a little over twice the number during the same period. Between 1981-87, the union membership increased by almost 8 times in public sector whereas it increased by 4 times in private sector.

The higher rate of increase in the degree of unionisation has a positive impact on strike activity in the public sector, during 1971-80. But during 1981-87, the strike activity has not increased in proportion with the degree of unionisation. In public sector both the number of unions and union membership increased by more than 7 times whereas the strike activity has increased by more than

5 times. The increase in degree of unionisation might be due to the establishment of big public sector organisation like National Aluminium Company Limited (NALCO) and Co-operative Spinning Mills has established its new divisional branches at different places which are also playing a positive role in controlling strike activity in both the sectors. The Government being an ideal employer, it is expected to provide better facilities to workers. But in practice, the management has not come up to meet the growing needs of the workers. Moreover, the unions are influenced by external forces. The intra-union rivalry is also a contributing factor in encouraging strike activity in both the sectors.

DISTRIBUTION OF STRIKES IN INDUSTRIES

To get a clear picture of strike activity, industry-wise distribution of strikes needs special attention. Concentration of work force in large industrial establishments, increase in the number of establishments, technological factors, and industrial environment all have a great impact on strike activity.

The table 2.18 gives the number and percentage distribution of strikes in the different industries (Industries have been classified in 17 groups). Industries like iron and steel, textile, transport, electricity, paper, aluminium, etc., which dominated stoppage statistics are analysed individually. The less affected industries like beedi and tobacco, rice and flour mills, etc., are grouped where necessary. The rarely affected industries are grouped together under the head "other industries".

This industry-wise analysis of strike activity in Orissa reveals that iron and steel, textiles, paper and paper products, electricity, transport and machine and machine products industry account for roughly 52 per cent of the total number of strikes. Out of a total of 8 strikes which occurred between 1964 and 1980, roughly 402 strikes took place in these seven industries. During 1981-89, the aluminium industry recorded about 7 per cent of the strikes. The other seven industries listed about accounted for 52 per cent of strike during 1964-80 and between 1981-89, it is more than 54 per cent.

Of these seven industries iron and steel alone accounted for roughly 15 per cent of the strikes. The textile industry comes next.

Table 2.18 Percentage Distribution of Strikes among Industries

Sl. No.	Industry	1964-70		1971-75		1976-80		1981-85		1986-89	
		No. of strikes	% of total strikes	No. of strikes	% of total strikes	No. of strikes	% of total strikes	No. of strikes	% of total strikes	No. of strikes	% of total strikes
1.	Iron and Steel	31	15.7	28	13.3	62	15.7	44	11.4	36	13.1
2.	Textile	18	09.1	24	11.4	31	07.8	32	08.6	25	09.12
3.	Transport	07	03.5	24	11.4	18	04.5	13	03.5	17	06.2
4.	Electricity	02	1.1	12	05.7	13	03.3	21	05.6	14	05.1
5.	Paper and paper products	20	10.1	16	07.6	48	12.2	17	4.5	13	04.7
6.	Cement	05	02.5	01	0.4	01	0.2	08	2.1	11	4.0
7.	Aluminium	04	02.03	03	1.4	06	1.5	23	6.1	22	8.0
8.	Ceramic and Refractories	05	2.5	7	3.3	10	2.5	13	3.5	7	2.5
9.	Electrical machine equipment	5	2.5	1	0.4	0	–	9	2.4	9	3.2

10. Machine and machine products	7	3.5	24	11.4	14	3.5	38	10.2	31	11.3
11. Chemical and Chemical Products	10	5.07	7	3.3	12	3.05	33	8.8	18	6.5
12. Glass	–	–	2	0.9	2	0.5	–	-	–	–
13. Beedi and Tobacco	5	2.5	–	-	1	–	–	–	–	–
14. Rice and Flour Mills	5	2.5	6	2.8	4	1.02	6	1.6	–	–
15. Sugar	–	–	–	–	2	0.5	–	–	1	0.3
16. Metal and Metal Products Ferro Alloys	6	3.04	6	2.8	13	3.3	28	7.5	16	5.8
17. Miscellaneous	67	34.01	51	24.2	185	47.00	86	23.1	65	23.7
Total	197	100	210	100	393	100	371	100	274	100

Source : Labour Directorate, Government of Orissa.

accounting for 9 per cent of the strikes. The analysis further shows that some industries like sugar, beedi and tobacco, glass making, etc. have been less affected by strikes. They account for only 2 per cent of the total number of strikes. Of these less affected industries sugar industry is rearely affected by strike activity. Table 2.18 gives the number and percentage distribution of strikes in the different industries. Between 1981-89, in beedi and tobacco and glass industry occurrence of strike is nil. Sugar is also rarely affected. Metal products registered more than seven per cent of the strike activity.

The findings of the above mentioned table are further supported by the data analysed in the table 2.19 which shows the ranking of different industries on the basis of strike frequency.

Table 2.19. Strike frequency ranking for industries (1964-89)

Sl. No.	*Industry*	*Total No. of strikes*	*Annual average*	*Ranking*
1.	Iron and Steel	195	7.5	1st
2.	Textile	124	4.7	2nd
3.	Machine and Machine. Products	113	4.3	3rd
4.	Paper and Paper Products	106	4.07	4th
5.	Transport	80	3.07	5th
6.	Chemical and Chemical Products	74	2.8	6th
7.	Metal and Metal Products	66	2.5	7th
8.	Aluminium	57	2.1	8th
9	Ceramic and Refractories	47	1.8	9th
10	Electricity	34	1.3	10th
11	Cement	26	1.0	11th
12	Electrical equipment	24	0.9	12th
13	Beedi and Tobacco	7	0.2	13th
14	Rice and Flour	6	0.23	14th
15	Sugar	1	0.03	15th
16	Glass	1	0/03	16th
17	Other Industries	459	17.6	—

Source: Labour Directorate, Government of Orissa

The possible explanations for the high strike frequency in Iron and Steel, Textile, Machine and Machine Products and Paper Products are:

(i) Size—Most of these units are relatively large in size. The Rourkela Steel Plant is the biggest industrial establishment in the State, employing more than 30 thousand people. Roughly 15 thousand persons are employed in Textile and Paper Industries.

(ii) Most of the units are multi-union units and are constantly facing the problem of inter and intra-union rivalry. The Rourkela Steel Plant has 13 unions.

(iii) Most of these plants are located in industrial centres like Chaudwar, Rourkela, etc. Hence, environmental factors also contribute to the higher strike frequency.

MAN-DAYS LOST INDUSTRY-WISE

The distribution of man-days lost gives a slightly different picture. Our earlier analysis has shown that in terms of strike frequency, iron and steel, textile occupy first and second places respectively. But the distribution of man-days lost industry-wise shows that paper and paper products and textile occupy first and second positions respectively. Paper and paper products accounts for roughly 13 per cent, textile 10 per cent of man-days lost. Iron and steel which occupies the first place in terms of strike frequency accounts for 7.3 per cent of man-days lost. Generation and distribution of electricity and machine making account for roughly 9 and 5 per cent of man-days lost respectively. Transport accounts for only 3 per cent of man-days lost. The industry-wise distribution of man-days lost is given below:

Table 2.20. Percentage of man-days lost industry-wise (1971-89)

Sl. No.	*Industry*	*Man-days lost*	*Percentage of total man-days lost*
1.	Iron and steel	275847	7.32
2.	Electricity	337212	8.9
3.	Textile	384399	10.2

4.	Transport	111484	2.9
5.	Paper and Paper Products	481946	12.8
6.	Chemical and Chemical Products	87746	2.3
7.	Machine and Machine Products	180844	4.8
8.	Ceramic and Refractories	83277	2.2
9.	Metal and Metal Products	70417	1.8
10.	Aluminium	145358	3.8
11.	Rice and Flour Mills	6835	0.1
12.	Beedi and Tobacco	463	0.01
13.	Electrical Mechanical equipment	29351	0.7
14.	Cement	38957	1.03
15.	Sugar	2442	0.06
16.	Glass	12426	0.33
17.	Other Industries	1515665	40.25
	Total	3764759	100

Source: Labour Directorate, Government of Orissa.

3

STRIKES BY PLANT SIZE

Man-days lost due to industrial action in Orissa as analysed in the previous chapters has shown an increase over a period of two decades. We have now to investigate whether all or the majority of plants are affected by strike activity or the strike activity is confined to a small proportion of plants.

An attempt has been made in this chapter to analyse this aspect and also to find out the salient features of strike affected plants, especially their size.

A study of registered factories in Orissa reveals a predominance of small plants. Out of 849 factories registered and operating with 10 and above workers during 1980 in Orissa, 711 or roughly 84 per cent of plants were employing less than 100 workers. Only 2.3 per cent of the factories were employing more than 500 workers per plant. Plants employing more than 5000 workers were only 2 in number which constituted less than one per cent of the total plants. In 1986, the analysis indicates that about 90 per cent of plants are employing less than 100 workers. The table 3.1 presents the classification of registered factories according to their size.

Table 3.1. Size-wise classification of registered factories in Orissa, 1980 and 1986

Plant size	*1980*		*1986*	
	Number	*Per cent*	*Number*	*Per cent*
10-24	396	46.6	637	49.3
25-99	315	30.7	524	40.5
100-199	71	8.3	59	4.5
200-499	38	4.4	39	3.2
500-999	15	1.7	16	1.2
1000-5000	12	1.5	13	1.0
5000 and above	2	0.3	3	0.2
Total	849		1291	

Source: The Office of the Chief Inspector of Factories and Boilers, Government of Orissa. Percentage calculated by the Researcher. Plants are classified on the basis of the number of workers employed.

PLANTS AFFECTED BY STRIKES

A study of plants affected by strike activity shows that on an average only 5 per cent of the total number of plants are affected by strike activity and 95 per cent remain unaffected by such activity. This means that by and large, the vast majority of plants in Orissa are free from strike action.

The percentage distribution of plants affected and unaffected by strike activity in Orissa between 1978 and 1986 is given below:

Table 3.2. Percentage distribution of strike affected/ unaffected plants

Nature of Plants	*1978*	*1979*	*1980*	*1986*	*Average*
Strike affected plants	3.1	3.7	5.2	7.7	4.9
Unaffected by strike activity	96.9	96.3	94.8	92.3	95.1

Source: The Labour Directorate, Government of Orissa.

The Table 3.2 shows that though on an average only 5 per cent of plants have been affected by strike activity, there is clearly an increasing trend in such activity. The percentage of plants affected by strike activity has increased from 3.1 per cent in 1978 to 5.2 per cent in 1980, and to 7.7 per cent in 1986. Within a period of six years 2.5 per cent increase in number of strike affected plants does not confirm a new trend.

Further analysis of the plants affected by strike activity shows that over the three years period 1978 to 80, roughly three fourths of the number of plants had experienced only one stoppage per year, and a very small proportion, say 2 per cent, had a larger number of stoppages due to strike. 17 per cent of the plants had an average of two strikes a year, and 7 per cent had 3 to 6 strikes a year. The distribution of affected plants on the basis of number of stoppages due to strike experienced by them in a year is given below.

Table 3.3. Percentage distribution of affected plants on the basis of number of stoppages due to strike

Plants affected	*Percentage*
1 Stoppage	74
2 Stoppages	17
3 To 6 Stoppages	7
4 Stoppages and above	2

Source:: The Labour Directorate, Government of Orissa.

STRIKE AFFECTED PLANTS ACCORDING TO SIZE

The percentage of plants affected by strike increases with size. Between 1978-80, on an average only 0.73 per cent of plants were strike affected in the 10-24 size whereas 64.2 per cent of plants with 1000 or more workers were strike affected. A continuously increasing trend is noticed with increase in the size of plant. The larger the plant, the greater is the probability of strikes. The Table 3.4 shows the percentage distribution of strike affected plants according to their size.

Table 3.4. Percentage distribution of plants affected by strikes

Size of Plants	*1978*	*1979*	*1980*	*Annual Average*
10-24	1.5	0.46	0.25	0.73
25-99	7.0	7.1	0.6	4.9
100-199	21.5	22.0	12.6	18.7
200-499	21.2	38.2	28.9	29.4
500-999	70.0	38.46	46.6	51.6
1000 and above	78.5	50.00	64.2	64.2

Source : The Labour Directorate, Government of Orissa.

STRIKES PER PLANT AGAINST PLANT SIZE

A second aspect of strike intensity is the direct relationship between the average number of strikes per plant per annum and the plant size. Strikes per plant per annum is minimum (numbering 0.005) in plants employing less than 25 workers and is maximum (numbering 11) in plants employing 5000 or more workers. The plants employing less than 500 workers experienced less than 1 strike (0.37) per plant per annum. But for plants employing from 500 to 5000 workers the number of strikes per plant per annum comes to roughly 1. This number all of a sudden increases to 11 for plants employing more than 5000 workers. Details of strikes per plant per annum for plants of different sizes are given in undermentioned table.

Table 3.5. Frequency of strikes per plant

Size	*Strike Per Plant*			*Annual Average*
	1978	*1979*	*1980*	
10-24	0.01	0.004	0.002	0.005
25-99	0.08	0.07	0.07	0.07
100-199	0.27	0.22	0.15	0.21
200-499	0.3	0.47	0.34	0.37
500-999	0.9	0.53	0.6	0.67
1000-5000	1.0	0.58	0.6	0.72
5000 & above	12.0	13.00	9.0	11.00

Source: The Labour Directorate, Government of Orissa.

It has been mentioned earlier that roughly three fourths of the number of plants experienced one stoppage a year between 1978 and 80 and only one fourth of them experienced more than one stoppage each year. The distribution of such plants on the basis of strike incidence and size of plant is given below.

Table 3.6. Percentage distribution of plants experiencing certain number of strikes

Size	*No. of Plants affected*	*1 Strike affected*	*2 Strike affected*	*3-6 Strike affected*	*7 or more Strike affected*
10-24	4	3 (75)	1 (25)	—	—
25-99	19	15 (79)	3 (16)	1 (5)	—
100-199	11	9 (82)	2 (18)	—	—
200-499	10	9 (90)	1 (10)	—	—
500-1000	7	5 (72)	1 (4)	1 (14)	—
1000 and above	9	4 (45)	2 (22)	2 (22)	1 (11)

Source: The Labour Directorate, Government of Orissa.

N. B.: Figures in brackets indicate percentage.

It will appear from the above table that roughly 79 per cent of plants employing less than 100 workers experienced only one stoppage a year, 17 per cent witnessed 2 stoppages per plant per year and only 4 per cent of the plants experienced from 3 to 6 stoppages per plant per year. But 56 per cent of the plants employing more than 500 workers experienced only one stoppage a year, the remaining 44 per cent of such plants witnessed 3 to 6 stoppages per plant per year. Thus, the analysis proves that the strike activity is concentrated mostly in large sized plants. A large number of such plants experience more than 2 stoppages each year.

MAN-DAYS LOST PER PLANT

Man-days lost per plant also show the same trend over three years. It increases with the increase in plant size. For plants employing less than 100 workers, the average loss of man- days per plant comes to roughly 36 days a year, whereas it is 273 for plants employing between 100 and 200 workers. It further increases to 3200 for plants employing 500 to 5000 workers, and for plants employing more than 5000 workers the average man-days lost per plant per year comes to roughly 6200 which is almost double the man-days lost in plants employing 500 to 5000 workers. This indicates that strike action imposes heavy burden in terms of man-days loss in larger size plants in comparison to smaller size plants. Details of average annual loss of man-days per plant per annum is given for different size of plants in the under- mentioned table:

Table 3.7. Man-days lost per plant

Size	*Strike Per Plant*			*Annual*
	1978	*1979*	*1980*	*Average*
10-24	1.4	1.76	0.06	1.07
25-99	42.8	49.00	14.9	35.50
100-199	389.4	238.20	193.6	273.40
200-499	887.7	1138.00	279.7	977.60
500-5000	3040.0	3588.90	3103.8	3244.20
5000 and above	9069.5	3180.00	6353.0	6208.80

Source: The Labour Directorate, Government of Orissa.

The above analysis of loss of working days shows a wide variation with establishments employing less than 500 workers and those having 500 or more workers. Nearly 978 working days are lost per plant with 200 to 499 workers whereas 3244 days are lost per plant with 500 to 5000 or more workers. Thus, establishments employing more than 500 workers bear a heavy loss of working days due to strikes.

MAN-DAYS LOST PER STRIKE

The Table No.3.7 has shown the annual loss of man-days per plant per year. The table given below shows man-days lost per strike in plants of different sizes. The number of man-days lost per strike varies on an average from 163 days for the plants of the lowest size (10-24) to 2381 days for the plants of a larger size (500 or more workers). The difference in loss of man-days is almost 15 times. This means that in large sized plants, strikes results in loss of more man-days than in small sized plants.

Table 3.8. Man-days lost per strike in different sized plants

Size	*Period*			*Annual Average*
	1978	*1979*	*1980*	
10-24	81.25	383.6	24.00	162.75
25-100	483.88	623.6	247.60	451.60
100-499	2048.16	1818.8	813.13	1559.03
500 and above	2069.55	2392.1	2680.00	2380.55

Source: The Labour Directorate, Government of Orissa.

STRIKERS PER STRIKE

The number of strikers per strike also varies with plant size. There is a gradual increase in the number of strikers per strike with plant size. The number of strikers per strike varies from 20(10-24) in the lower size range to 402 in higher size range (500 and above). There is almost a 20 times increase in the average number of strikers in plants having 500 or more workers over plants with 10 to 24 workers. Table 3.9 gives the number of strikers per strike in plants of different sizes.

Table 3.9. Strikers per strike against plant size

Plant Size	*Years*			*Annual Average*
	1978	*1979*	*1980*	
10-24	18	29	12	20
25-99	37	40	47	41
100-500	107	116	142	122
500 above	607	244	355	402

Source: The Labour Directorate, Government of Orissa.

STRIKES PER THOUSAND WORKERS

Strikes per thousand workers, another important indicator of strike measure, show a gradually increasing trend with plant size. Table 3.10 provides some explanation.

Table 3.10. Strikes per thousand workers

Plant Size	*1978*	*1979*	*1980*	*Annual Average*
10-24	0.002	0.002	0.0005	0.0015
25-99	0.006	0.005	0.003	0.0046
100-199	0.025	0.018	0.03	0.03
200-499	0.03	0.02	0.04	0.03
500 and above	0.07	0.05	0.05	0.05

Source: The Labour Directorate, Government of Orissa.

The above table shows that strikes per thousand workers per plant is 0.0015 in the lowest size range (10-24) and it is 0.05 in plants with 500 and above workers. Strikes per thousand workers increase as plant size increases. It is 0.03 for plants employing 100 to 500 workers.

It is clear from the table 3.10 analysis that strikes impose heavy burden on large plants. The chances of having a strike-free year is less for the larger plants. The percentage of workers affected by strikes increases with plant size and the expected number of strikes per year also increases with the increase in plant size.

It may be concluded from table 3.10 that strike intensity is a correlate of plant size.

But the real burden imposed by strikes on large plants can't be properly assessed unless the participation rate (strikers per thousand workers) and the striker days (loss of man-days per striker) are studied against plant size. A frequent occurrence of strikes may be expected in large plants, but a lower proportion of workers may be on strike at one time or there may be a tendency for strikes in large plants to be of shorter duration. Both the propositions may be true. An attempt is made here to examine the validity of these two propositions.

LOSS OF WORKING DAYS PER STRIKER

Table 3.11 summarises the loss of working days per striker.

Table 3.11. Loss of working days per striker for different plant size

Plant Size	*Year*			*Annual Average*
	1978	*1979*	*1980*	
10-99	11.9	28.7	5.2	15.2
100-499	19.2	16.6	5.7	13.5
500-1000	3.1	2.2	15.8	7.03
1000-5000	3.9	4.15	5.3	4.45
5000 and above	2.8	2.6	2.4	2.4

Source: The Labour Directorate, Government of Orissa.

The table above shows that the loss of working days per striker decreases with plant size. It varies from 15.2 days per striker in establishments employing less than 100 workers to 2.4 days per striker in plants having 5000 and above workers. In small establishments, loss of working days per striker is almost seven times more than in large sized establishments. In the case of establishments employing 100 to 500 workers, the loss of working days per striker is 13.5 days, which further decreases to 7.03 in establishments employing 500 to 1000 workers. The above table thus supports the proposition that strikes in the larger plants are usually of shorter duration, while those in smaller plants are of longer duration.

STRIKERS PER THOUSAND WORKERS

Table 3.12 gives the number of strikers per thousand workers.

Table 3.12. Strikers per thousand workers

Plant Size	*Year*			*Annual Average*
	1978	*1979*	*1980*	
10-24	891	720	800	804
25-99	936	430	990	785
100-199	924	773	587	761
200-499	571	779	923	753

500-999	885	668	520	691
1000-5000	588	428	235	417
5000 and above	220	57	121	133

Source: The Labour Directorate, Government of Orissa.

The above table shows that the strikers' participation rate also varies with plant size. The larger plants have the lower proportion of workers on strike while in small plants a higher proportion of workers participate in strike activity. The number of strikers per thousand workers varies from 804 on an average in the lower sized plants to 133 in plants having 5000 and above workers. Participation rate gradually decreases in plants having a comparatively larger number of workers. Plants with (10-24) workers have 804 strikers on an average per thousand workers whereas the larger plants have only 133 strikers per thousand workers. The number of strikers per thousand workers is 761 in plants employing 100 to 200 workers and only 417 in plants employing 100 to 5000 workers. The above analysis thus proves the second hypothesis that workers participation rate in strike activity decreases as the plant size increases. Participation rate is very high in small plants and it is low in large plants. The chances of cohesiveness among workers in small plants is much greater than in large sized plants. Again, regularity in a higher participation rate in strike activity is also. noticed in small sized plants.

On the basis of above analysis of strikes and plant size, it may be concluded that:

(i) a very small proportion of plants are affected by strike activity.

(ii) the larger the plant size, the greater is the possibility of strike.

(iii) large plants have frequent strikes.

(iv) worker participation rate in strike activity is low in large sized plants and high in small sized plants.

(v) strikes in small sized plants last longer than in large sized plants.

"The bigger the crowd, the greater is the chance of disagreement", might not be the only satisfactory explanation of this hypothesis. The larger the plant the greater is the probability of disagreement, hence more strikes. The communication gap between the managerial people and the employees, technological factors, and diversified nature of work might be the cause of more frequent outbreak of conflict in large plants than in small plants. In large plants, apart from the common grievances, different sections of people face different types of problems. Large plants, therefore experience departmental strikes.

The Rourkela Steel Plant, the biggest plant of the State and one of the biggest public sector undertakings of the country, employs more than 35,000 men. It did not experience a single general strike between 1978 and 80. But this single plant has experienced 59 departmental strikes during 1978-80; out of the 283 strikes recorded for the State. This comes to roughly 21 per cent of the total number of strikes in the State (1978-80). Again these 59 strikes were only departmental strikes with a very low participation rate and the short duration.

Table 3.13. Loss of working days per striker and strikers per thousand employees in the Rourkela Steel Plant during the 1970's

Year	*Loss of working days per striker*	*Striker per thousand employees*
1971	1.3	47
1972	3.4	9
1973	4.5	20
1974	1.1	100
1975	2.1	13
1976	—	—
1977	1.3	38
1978	4.9	94
1979	1.4	74
1980	3.0	120
Average	2.3	52

Source: (i) The Labour Directorate, Government of Orissa.
(ii) Offical records of the Rourkela Steel Plant.

Data analysed in table 3.13 show that man-days lost per striker was 2.3 on an average during the 1970's and on an average 52 strikers per thousand employees participated in strike activity. The loss of man-days per striker was a minimum of 1.1 days in 1974 and a minimum of 4.5 days in 1973. The number of strikers per thousand employees has varied from a minimum of 9 in 1972 to a maximum of 120 in 1980. This clearly shows that strikes in large plants are of short duration and have a low participation rate.

UNIONS AND STRIKE FREQUENCY

The given table 3.14 shows that strikes per plant increase as unions per plant increase both against plant size.

Table 3.14. Unions per plant and strikes per plant

Plant Size	*1978*		*1979*		*1980*		*1978-80 Annual Average*	
	Union	*Strike*	*Union*	*Strike*	*Union*	*Strike*	*Union*	*Strike*
10-99	0.33	0.03	0.37	0.03	0.38	0.2	0.36	0.026
100-499	2.36	0.28	2.3	0.03	2.15	0.27	0.27	0.19
500-999	3.90	0.9	3.4	0.53	3.13	0.6	3.47	0.67
1000-5000	4.0	1.0	3.5	0.58	0.75	0.6	3.75	0.72
5000 and above	18.0	12.0	19.0	13.0	19.0	9.0	18.83	11.0

Source: The Labour Directorate, Government of Orissa..

The above table reveals that small sized plants have less than one union per plant while large sized plants are usually multi-union plants. Plants employing less than 100 workers are usually single-union plants, but others are multi-union plants. Among such plants the number of unions per plant is the highest, roughly 19 for plants employing more than 5000 workers whereas it is roughly 2 in plants employing more than 100 but less than 500 employees. For other plants, unions per plant come up to be a little more than 3.

When strike activity in these multi-union plants are analysed, it will appear that plants having more than 2 unions have witnessed more strikes per annum than plants having less than two unions. In single union plants, the average number of strikes per annum per plant come to only 0.026, whereas in plants having more than 18 unions, the average number of strikes per annum per plant rises to roughly 11. In plants having 3 or 4 unions, the average number of strikes per year per plant came to 0.67 and 0.72 respectively. Again, the Rourkela Steel Plant, which is a multi-union plant with 14 unions has witnessed roughly 20 strikes per year between 1978 and 80.

It is thus clear that multi-union plants on an average face more strikes per annum than single union plants. In multi-union plants, many of the strikes are caused by intra-union and inter- union rivalries.

Again in large sized plants, the workers have greater expectations and also more problems. The other possible reason for the greater incidence of strikes might be the fact that plants employing 100 or more men have to conform to the Industrial Employment (Standing Orders) Act, 1946 which regulates employment conditions. If there is the least violation of service conditions by the employer, the workers at once resort to strike. But in small establishments the unions are often weak, their service conditions are not so well protected as those of the employees of the large and medium sized establishments.

The other aspect of strike activity in the large plants is that a lower proportion of employees is on strike at any time and the strikes are of shorter duration. It has been mentioned in one of the earlier pages that the large plants are usually multi- union plants. As such, strikes declared by a union generally do not get the support of workers belonging to the rival unions. Again, in large sized plants, different departments have their individual problems which may not affect the workers of other departments. In such cases departmental strikes which are very common in larg plants do not always find the support of all the workers of the plant. Such strikes get full support from the workers of that department only. Moreover, in many cases departmental strikes are declared without prior consultation with the unions. This explains the low participation rate in strike activity in large plants. For instance, in the Rourkela Steel Plant, all the 59 strikes which took place between 1978 and 80 were departmental strikes. Of these 59 strikes, 17 were declared without the consent of the trade unions. Again, if participation rate is calculated on plant-wise basis, the number of strikers per 1000 employees comes to only 120. But if participation rate is calculated department wise, it comes to 793 per thousand employees of the striking department. The necessary data are given in under mentioned table 3.15.

Table 3.15. Strikers per thousand employees against the plant and strike affected department during 1980 in the Rourkela Steel Plant.

Total employees of the plant	38,589
Total number of employees of the strike affected departments	5,771
Number of strikers	4,574
Strikers per thousand employees	120
Strikers per thousand employees (against Strike affected department)	793

Source: (i) The Labour Directorate, Government of Orissa.
(ii) Offical Records of the Rourkela Steel Plant.

It has been mentioned earlier that strikes in large plants are usually shorter in duration. A two-fold explanation may be given for this particular phenomenon:

(i) Even departmental strikes in large plants attract the attention of all the political parties including the State Government. This immediately activates the State Industrial Relations Machinery and the process of settlement starts immediately.

(ii) Moreover, these plants have usually strong unions; hence management, too, instead of adopting a policy of "Wait and See" immediately makes strenuous efforts to bring about some amicable settlement.

SUMMARY

To summarise the discussions in this chapter, the following may be stated:

1. Roughly 96 per cent of plants in Orissa remain free from strike action.
2. The larger the plant size, the greater is the possibility of strike.
3. Large plants witness frequent strikes.
4. Employees, participation rate is low in large sized plants and high in small sized plants.
5. Workers militancy is more in small sized plants, as strikes in such plants are usually of longer duration.

4

DISTRIBUTION OF STRIKES BY CAUSES

The general nature of strike activity-its trend and its industry-wise, sector-wise and plant-wise distribution has been analysed in the previous chapters. It provides only a broad idea of the pattern of strike activity in Orissa. It does not provide answers to many pertinent questions like, why strikes occur, who sponsor the strikes, how long strikes continue, what is the participation rate and a number of other questions. An attempt has been made in this chapter to examine some of these issues.

WHY STRIKES OCCUR?

This particular question needs both a macro and a micro analysis of strike activity in Orissa.

Undoubtedly, strike is an overt expression of the dissatisfaction of the work force, which may be caused by a number of factors like demand for an increase in wages, payment of bonus, reduction of working hours, improvement in working conditions, recognition of unions, intra-union rivalry, changes in service conditions, retrenchment, protest against disciplinary action, unfair treatment by supervisors, etc. Sometimes strikes occur when either party fails to implement the terms of a settlement, or if they even refuse to negotiate a dispute. At times, union leaders organise strikes to prove their leadership quality and strength.

Very often, strikes are the result of continuous discontentment over a period of time. In such cases the immediate reasons given for the strike may not be the real cause. Usually a strike is a complex phenomenon having a mixture of causes, hence selection of any one cause may be somewhat arbitrary. This particular phenomenon thus calls for a macro and micro analysis.

It is also significant that the nature of demand changes over the passage of time. Ross and Hartman,[1] B.C. Roberts,[2] and Knowles[3] have found that the nature of demand changes over time. In the early period of industrialization, strikes represented a revolt against the established authority represented by an employer. However, strikes now have tended to be more of a protest and demonstration without any overt or covert intention of subverting the authority of the State or of an employer. Again, wages and allowances which generally predominated during the early period of industrialization gave way to status, union recognition of personnel problems during later part, when industrialization achieved a fairly high degree of maturity. Employees, once they find that their biological needs are met, look towards fulfilment of needs for security, status, etc. This particular character of humar nature causes a change in strike demands.

In a developing economy like ours, strikes for higher wages constitute the major part of industrial action. An appraisal of the trend in man-days lost reveals that between the year of independence and the First Five Year Plan (1951-56) when the real earnings of industrial workers were below the 1939 level, the loss of man-days was the maximum. On an average, 11.3 million man-days were lost per annum between 1946 and 1950. The improvement in real wages brought in the years of the First Plan seems to have had a salutary effect on industrial harmony; the loss was on an average only 3.9 million man-days per annum. Between the Second Plan and the first four years of the Third Plan, there was a fall in real earnings. The time loss was higher than what was witnessed in the First Plan, but much below that in the years prior to 1950. The real wages showed a downward trend for the two years thereafter. The spurt in the price level in 1967 eroded the real wages further. The years 1966 and 1967 saw a deterioration in the industrial harmony with the time loss per annum averaging much higher than in any of the years between 1956 and 1965.

Thus real wages of industrial workers largely influence strike activity and thus the industrial relation situation of the country. In other words it may be said that wages and related matters constitute the basic issues of strike and dominate the scene. Smith, Richard, Clifton, and others[5] have found wages as the dominating issue in strike activity in Great Britain.

Against this background, the distribution of strikes by causes in Orissa are analysed for the years 1964 to 89. The reasons for strike are classified under different heads like :

(1) Wages and allowances
(2) Bonus
(3) Personnel matters
(4) Leave and hours of work
(5) Charter of demands
(6) Other matters.

Personnel matters include job security, promotion, transfer, disciplinary measures, protest against misbehaviour of management, layoff and retrenchment. Strikes on trade union issues, sympathetic strikes and unspecified issues are included under "other matters".

CAUSE-WISE DISTRIBUTION OF STRIKES

The cause-wise distribution of strikes in Orissa between 1964 and 89 is given in table 4.1.

Table 4.1. Cause-wise distribution of strikes in India

Period	*Total No. of strikes*	*Wages and allowance*	*Bonus*	*Charter of demands*	*Personnel*	*Leave and hours of works*	*Other matters*
1964-67	143	44 (30.7)	13 (19.09)	19 (13.2)	46 (32.09)	7 (4.8)	14 (9.7)
1968-71	86	24 (27.9)	5 (5.8)	21 (24.4)	23 (26.7)	6 (6.9)	7 (8.1)

1972-75	183	66	2	36	64	5	10
		(36.6)	(1.09)	(19.6)	(34.9)	(2.7)	(5.4)
1976-80	393	73	32	98	142	16	32
		(18.8)	(8.1)	(24.9)	(36.1)	(4.07)	(8.1)
1981-85	371	87	10	103	109	7	43
		(23.4)	(2.6)	(27.7)	(29.3)	(5.9)	(11.5)
1986-89	286	60	8	95	71	22	30
		(20.9)	(2.7)	(33.2)	(24.8)	(7.6)	(10.4)
	1462	354	70	372	455	63	136
		(24.2)	(4.7)	(25.4)	(31.12)	(4.3)	(9.3)

Source: (i) Labour Directorate, Government of Orissa (Data have been collected from the official records of the Labour Directorate).
(ii) Percentage has been calculated by the researcher.

N. B.: Figures within bracket indicate percentage.

This analysis reveals that between 1964 and 89 personnel matters and wages including allowances were the two most important causes of strike in Orissa. Taken together, they accounted for roughly 60 per cent of strikes. Strikes on personnel issues varied from a minimum of 26.7 per cent during 1968-71 to 36.1 per cent during 1976-80 which was highest and 29.3 during 1981-85 and 24.8 between 1986-89. Similarly, strikes on wages and allowances have varied between 18.8 per cent during 1976-80 to 36.6 per cent during 1972-75. Charter of demands was the third important cause of strike, accounting for roughly 25 per cent of the total number of strikes. Between 1964 and 1980, strikes on charter of demands have increased from 13 per cent during 1964-67 to 25 per cent between 1976–80 and 33 per cent during 1986–89. Bonus was accounted for 7 per cent of the total number of strikes in Orissa during 1964–80, which reduced to roughly 5 per cent during 1964–89. Leave and hours of work stood almost at the bottom accounting for only 4 per cent of the strikes. Other questions like union issues, sympathetic strikes etc. on an average accounted for 9 per cent of the strikes during the period under study. It is interesting to mention here that strike on trade union issues there was hardly any strike in Orissa during sixties and in the early part of the seventies. But in the latter part of the seventies, strikes on trade union issue became frequent. During 1980's on an average one strike per year on trade union issues and one on assault by the management occurred in Orissa.

Again, if strike data are analysed on decadal basis it will appear that during the 1960s, strikes on wage issues were roughly 32 per cent which came down to 24 per cent during the 1970s. But, strikes on personnel matters increased by 4 per cent i.e. from 31 per cent during sixties to 35 per cent in the seventies. Strikes on charter of demands decreased from 24.2 per cent during the 1960's to 23 per cent during the 1970's. During 1980's, strikes on wage issues decreased by 2 per cent and on personnel issues by 3 per cent and increased by 7 per cent in case of charter of demands. Even though the proportion of strike on wage issues and personnel matters have declined between 1960-89, these three issues namely wages, personnel and charter of demands have remained the dominant causes of strikes in Orissa.

Distribution of strikes on wage issues, personnel matters and charter of demands on decadal basis is given in the table 4.2.

Table 4.2. Distribution of strikes on wage issue personnel matters and charter of demands during 1960's and 1970's

Period	*Total No. of strikes*	*Wage issues*	*Personnel matters*	*Charter of demands*
1960's	202	64 (31.6)	63 (31.1)	49 (24.2)
1970's	603	145 (24.04)	212 (35.1)	139 (23.15)
1980's	657	147 (22.3)	180 (27.3)	198 (30.1)

Source: (i) Labour Directorate, Government of Orissa
(ii) Percentage has been calculated by the researcher.

N. B.: Figures within bracket indicate percentage.

The relative importance of each cause can best be studied from the annual average number of strikes relating to different causes during the sixties, the seventies and eighties.

Table 4.3 explains that wages and allowances occupied the first position during 1964-69 and 1970-75 but 3rd position during 1980's with an annual average of 11, 16 and 15 strikes respectively. Personnel matters during these periods were responsible for an average of 9 and 13 strikes respectively and occupied the second rank. But in the latter part of the seventies i.e. between 1976 and 80

Table 4.3 : Average number of strikes on different causes

Causes	1964-69 annual average number	Ranking order	1970-75 annual average number	Ranking order	1976-80 annual average number	Ranking order	1981-85 annual average number	Ranking order	1986-89 annual average number	Ranking order
1. Wages and allowances	11	I	16	I	21	II	17	III	15	III
2. Personnel	9	II	13	II	28	I	22	I	18	II
3. Charter of demand	4	III	8	III	19	III	21	II	24	I
4. Other issues	2	IV	3	IV	5	IV	8	IV	8	IV
5. Leave and hours of work	1	V	2	V	3	V	1	V	3	V
6. Trade union issues	—	VI	—	VI	1	VI	1	VI	1	VI

Source: The Labour Directorate, Government of Orissa.

and during 1981-85, occupied first position. Strike on wages and allowances were relegated to the second position with 21 average annual strikes and strikes in personnel were elevated to the first position with an average annual of 28 strikes during 1976-80 but between 1981-89, strikes on wage issues relegated to 3rd position whereas personnel matters continue to occupy first position between 1981-85 and second position between 1986-89. Charter of demands continued to occupy the third position throughout 1969's-70's, with an annual average of 4, 8 and 19 strikes respectively, but during 1980's, it continued to occupy Ist position.

This shows that these three issues were the main causes of all strikes.

ECONOMIC AND NON-ECONOMIC ISSUES

When the various causative factors are classified under economic and non-economic, a very interesting picture emerges.

The classification of strikes on the basis of economic and non-economic issues is given below:

Table 4.4. Distribution of strikes on economic and non-economic issues during 1960's, 1970's and 1980's

Period	*Total strikes*	*Economic*	*Non-economic*
1960's	202	116 (57.4)	86 (42.6)
1970's	603	319 (52.9)	284 (47.1)
1980's	657	363 (55.2)	294 (45.8)
	1462	798 (54.5)	684 (45.5)

Source: (i) Labour Directorate, Government of Orissa.
N. B. Under economic cause, wages and allowances, bonus and charter of demands are included 99% of the charter of demands include economic demand and others.

Table 4.4 explains that out of every 100 strikes, 54 strikes occurred on economic issues like additional wages and allowances, higher rates of bonus etc., and 46 strikes occurred over non-economic issues like personnel and other issues.

Further, both during the Sixties, the Seventies and Eighties economic issues remained the most effective cause of strike accounting for 57 per cent, 53 and 55 per cent of strikes respectively. But strikes on non-economic issues had increased at a much faster rate than those on economic issues. Strikes over non-economic issues which had accounted for only 43 per cent of strikes during sixties, accounted for 47 per cent of strikes during the seventies and 45 per cent during eighties.

MAN-DAYS LOST

Man-days lost on economic and non-economic issues also show that a greater proportion of working days lost was accounted for by economic issues.

The analysis reveals three important features of man-days lost due to strike. They are:

(1) Between 1971 and 80, nearly 53 per cent of man-days lost was on account of strikes on economic issues and 47 per cent on non- economic issues.

(2) During the early years of the seventies more man-days were lost on account of strikes on non-economic issues. But from 1974 onwards the trend reversed; more man-days were lost due to strikes on economic issues and loss on non-economic issues.

(3) During 1979 and 1980 more than 85 per cent of man-days lost was on account of strikes on economic issues and approximately 15 per cent on non-economic issues.

The table below shows loss of man-days on economic and non- economic issues during 1971-80.

Table 4.5. Loss of man-days on economic and non-economic issues during 1971-80

Period	*Total Man-days lost*	*Man-days lost on economic issue*	*Man-days lost on non-economic issue*	*Percentage*	
				Economic	*Non-economic*
1971	1,30,008	14,818	1,15,190	11.4	86.6
1972	1,60,438	75,027	85,411	48.2	51.8
1973	1,48,855	37,942	1,10,943	25.4	74.6
1974	2,63,220	1,47,792	1,15,428	56.1	43.9
1975	2,97,051	1,40,942	1,52,577	44.0	56.0
1976	14,989	6,006	8,983	40.0	60.0
1977	3,44,618	2,44,081	1,00,537	70.0	30.0
1978	1,88,266	1,24,064	64,202	77.5	32.5
1979	2,91,680	2,85,896	5,784	89.1	10.9
1980	1,63,663	1,37,004	26,659	83.7	16.3
	20,02,788	10,65,750	9,37,038	53.2	47.0

N. B. Economic issue includes wages and allowances, bonus and charter of demands.

Table 4.6 shows the loss of man-days on economic and non- economic issues between 1981-89.

Table 4.6. Loss of man-days on economic and non-economic issues during 1980's

Period	*Total Man-days lost*	*Man-days lost on economic issue*	*Man-days lost on non-economic issue*	*Percentage*	
				Economic	*Non-economic*
1981	2,73,380	63,114	2,10,266	23.08	76.02
1982	1,18,200	55,523	62,677	46.9	53.1
1983	4,21,744	4,10,591	11,153	97.3	2.7
1984	2,42,560	82,009	1,60,551	33.8	66.2
1985	2,48,637	87,396	1,61,241	35.1	64.9
1986	2,44,579	95,147	1,49,372	38.9	61.1
1987	3,21,168	1,37,905	1,83,263	42.9	57.1
1988	1,62,255	1,14,970	47,285	70.8	29.2
1989	4,41,410	2,73,331	1,68,079	61.9	39.1
Total	22,27,873	13,19,986	9,07,887	59.2	40.8

N. B. Economic issues includes wages and allowances, bonus and charter of demands.

During 1980's high percentage of man-days lost was recorded on economic issues. Between 1980-81 about 60 per cent of man-days were lost in economic strikes and 40 per cent in non-economic strikes. The analysis reveals a different trend in 1981, 1983 and 1988. In the year 1981 only 23 per cent of loss was caused by strikes on economic demands and 76 per cent loss was due to strikes on non-economic demands. In the year 1983, more than 97 per cent of man-days loss was due to strikes on economic issues. In the year 1988, the percentage of loss was also more than 70% in case of economic strikes.

In the year 1983 the high percentage of loss was attributed by a prolonged strike on the demand of bonus in Orient Paper Mills, Brajrajnagar (Sambalpur district). That single strike caused a loss of 3,60,580 man-days.

Among the economic issues, pay increase was the single largest cause of strike. Other causes like non-payment of increased wages, non-implementation of wage board recommendations, bonus, non-payment of additional dearness allowances and grant of fringe benefits etc. have also caused strike.

Table 4.7 summarises the nature of economic demands and strikes caused by them during 1964-89.

Table 4.7. Distribution of strikes on economic causes

Period	*Total No. of economic Strikes*	*Wage increase*	*Non-payment of increased wages*	*Non-implementation of wage Board Recommendation*	*Bonus*	*Other issues*
1964-67	76	35 (47.05)	10 (13.1)	1 (1.3)	17 (22.3)	13 (17.1)
1968-71	50	25 (52.0)	5 (10.0)	11 (22.0)	5 (10.0)	3 (6.0)
1972-75	104	69 (66.3)	5 (4.08)	3 (2.8)	2 (1.9)	25 (24.3)
1976-80	205	120 (58.5)	19 (9.2)	1 (0.04)	32 (16.09))	32 (25.6)
1981-85	129	74 (57.3)	15 (11.6)	5 (3.8)	9 (6.9)	26 (20.1)
1986-89	102	58 (56.8)	13 (12.7)	2 (1.9)	7 (6.8)	19 (18.6)
	666	382 (57.3)	67 (10.06)	23 (3.4)	68 (10.2)	141 (21.1)

Source: (i) Labour Directorate, Government of Orissa
(ii) Percentage has been calculated by the researcher.

N. B.: Figures within bracket indicate percentage.

Table 4.7 explains that during 1964-89 roughly 55 per cent of the strikes on economic issues were declared on pay increase. The strikers wanted an increase in their basic pay. Roughly 10 per cent of the strikes were declared on bonus, and 10 per cent of the strikes were on non-payment of increased wages. Strikes on non-implementation of Wage Board recommendations constituted roughly 3 per cent of the strikes; 21 per cent of the strikes were caused over other economic issues like, compensation, funeral benefits, dearness allowances, additional dearness allowance increments, etc. Thus pay increase together with non-payment of increased pay accounted for roughly three-fourth of the number of strikes on economic issues. Hence the age-old finding that wages themselves are the single greatest cause of strike in India is proved by the above analysis.

Periodic analysis shows that throughout the period of analysis more than 47 per cent of the strikes were declared on pay issue. During 1972-75, 69 per cent of the strikes declared on economic issues were on increase in pay. During the last part of the 1970's strikes on pay increase decreased by 12 per cent. This periodic fluctuation was related to the cost of living index.

Strikes for non-payment of increased wages constituted 13 per cent of the total number of strikes on economic issues, between 1964-67. During the early part of the 1970's only 4 per cent of strikes were declared on this issue. But during the last part of the seventies this number rose to 9 per cent of the strikes on economic issues. During 1980's it increased to 12 per cent.

Strikes on non-implementation of Wage Board recommendations were negligible in number. Little more than one per cent of strikes on economic issues were declared on non-implementation of Wage Board recommendations during 1964-67. Again during the last part of the seventies, only one strike was declared on this issue, which is less than one per cent of the strikes on economic issues. During 1980's also the percentage varies between 11 to 2.5 per cent. But the period 1968-71 recorded 22 per cent of the economic strikes on non-implementation of Wage Board recommendations. The reason for this sudden spurt in strike activity on this account was that the recommendations of Wage Boards for cement, sugar, and a few other industries were awaiting implementation of their decisions regarding wage fixation in different units of the concerned industries.

Strikes on bonus issue constituted more than 22 per cent of the strikes on economic issues during 1964-67. It decreased to 10 per cent during 1968-71 and further to 2.1 per cent during 1972-75. It is interesting to note that its proportion again increased to 16 per cent during the last part of the 1970's. During 1980's roughly 7 per cent of strikes were declared on bonus issues.

Decrease and increase in strike activity on bonus, non- payment of increased wages, non-implementation of Wage Board recommendatiaons appear to have been influenced by the legislative enactments and recommendations of the tripartite bodies like the Wage Board.

Decadal analysis of strikes on economic issues showed that during the 1960's strike for higher pay were roughly 41 per cent, which increased to 63 per cent during the 1970's. Strikes for non-payment of increased wages, bonus and other related issues declined during the 1970's. The table below shows the decade-wise trend of strikes on economic issues.

Table 4.8. Distribution of strikes on economic issues during 1960's, 1970's and 1980's

Period	*Total strikes on economic issue*	*Wage increase*	*Non-payment of increased wages*	*Non-implemen tation of wage board Recom-mendation*	*Bonus*	*Other issue*
1960's	116	48 (41.3)	14 (12.07)	4 (3.4)	17 (14.6)	33 (28.4)
1970's	319	202 (63.3)	25 (7.5)	12 (3.7)	35 (10.9)	45 (14.1)
1980's	231	132 (57.4)	28 (12.1)	7 (3.03)	16 (6.9)	45 (19.4)
Total	666	382 (57.3)	67 (10.06)	23 (3.4)	68 (10.2)	141 (21.1)

Source: (i) Labour Directorate, Government of Orissa
(ii) Percentage has been calculated by the researcher.

N. B.: Figures within bracket indicate percentage.

Further analysis showed that per year on an average 7 strikes were declared on pay-increase during the sixties which increased to 20 during the seventies. The table below gives the annual average of strikes on wage increase and economic issues during the sixties, seventies and eighties.

This table explains that the annual average number of strikes on economic issues increased less than two times during the 1970's in comparison to the 1960's, where strikes for higher pay increased roughly three times. During 1980's strikes on pay issues increased by two times. It is thus clear from the above analysis that in Orissa, economic issues were the dominant cause of strikes. Among economic issues, demand for higher pay including payment of enhanced pay/dearness allowances, etc. were the principal cause of strike activity. But the important point of the analysis was that strikes on economic issues tended to decrease over the decades whereas non-economic issues tended to increase. Strikes on wage increase issue increased by more than 20 per cent during the seventies in comparison to the sixties. During 1980's strikes on pay issues increased by 13 per cent when compared with 1960's but it decreased by 9 per cent in comparison to the seventies.

Table 4.9. Decade-wise trend of strikes on economic issues and issues on higher wages during 1960's and 1970's

Total	*Annual average of strikes on economic issues*	*Annual average of strikes on pay issues*	*Percentage of strikes on pay issues and economic issues*
1960's	17	7	41.00
1970's	32	20	63.00
1980's	26	14	54.00

PERSONNEL-AN IMPORTANT ISSUE OF STRIKE ACTIVITY

During the period for which this analysis has been made strikes on personnel issues varied from 27 per cent to 36 per cent. On an average 16 strikes per year were caused on personnel issues. During the sixties personnel matters resulted in an average of 9 strikes per year, which was 21 during the 1970's and 20 during 1980's.

Personnel issues include factors like retrenchment, protest against disciplinary action, protest against misbehaviour of the management, and job conditions relating to promotion, transfer, service rules, etc.

The Table 4.10 summarises the distribution of strikes on personnel issues.

Among personnel issues, strike demands on job conditions constituted the majority. Between 1964-80 more than 50 per cent of the strike on personnel issues were exclusively on job conditions like personnel policy. On an average 8 strikes per year were caused over job conditions. But during 1980's only 40 per cent strikes were declared on job conditions : on an average 8 strikes per year were caused over this issue.

Table 4.10. Distribution of strikes on personnel issues

Period	*Total No. Strikes*	*Retrenchment*	*Protest against disciplinary action*	*Protest against misbehaviour of management*	*Job conditions*
1964-67	46	5 (10.8))	12 (26.0)	2 (4.3)	27 (58.6)
1968-71	23	3 (13.0)	6 (26.0)	1 (4.3)	13 (56.5)
1972-75	64	13 (20.3)	14 (21.8)	4 (6.2)	33 (51.5)
1976-80	142	14 (9.8)	33 (23.2)	20 (14.08)	75 (52.8)
1981-85	109	22 (20.1)	34 (31.1)	13 (11.9)	40 (36.6)
1986-89	71	19 (26.7)	31 (43.6)	3 (4.2)	33 (46.4)
	455	76 (16.7)	130 (28.5)	43 (9.4)	221 (48.5)

Source: (i) Labour Directorate, Government of Orissa

The next important issue was the protest against disciplinary action, occupying the second position in the incidence of strikes with 20 to 43 per cent of the strikes being on personnel issues. Strikes on this issue increased by 20 per cent between 1976-89. Retrenchment occupied the third position with roughly 17 per cent of strikes. During the period of analysis the percentage varies between 10 and 26 per cent. Protest against misbehaviour of management constituted the lowest percentage which varied from 4 to 14 per cent. On an average more than one strike was declared every year as a protest against the misbehaviour of the management. Strikes on this particular issue have been showing a rising trend. During the early part of the 1960's out of 100 strikes on personnel issues, only 4 strikes were related to misbehaviour of management, which increased to 14 during the last part of the 1970's. During 1980's out of 100 roughly 9 strikes were caused by the protest for misbehaviour of management.

From this analysis six pertinent points emerged which need some explanation:

(1) Workers' grievances over economic matters were a dominating issue in strike action.

(2) Higher wage was the main rallying cry of the workers.

(3) Workers' grievances were aggravated during this particular period by non-payment of wages and bonus, and non-implementation of Wage Board recommendations.

(4) Workers' dissatisfaction on personnel policy matters caused many strikes.

(5) Economic demands were decreasing over the decades whereas strike demands on personnel issues were rising.

(6) Strike caused due to protest againt disciplinary action and misbehaviour of management are increasing over the decades.

STRIKE ACTIVITY FOR HIGHER WAGES

The economic interest of an individual is the pivot around which all other interests revolve. In the words of A.S. Maslow[6], an individual first tries to satisfy his basic needs. After the basic needs are satisfied he thinks of a higher order of needs like social status, recognition, etc. Money plays a vital role in the fulfilment of the basic needs of an individual. The worker as an individual wants to be economically stable and feed himself and his family. To the wage earners and salaried persons the monthly pay is the principal source of income for the fulfilment of their basic needs like food, shelters, etc. Dissatisfaction begins the moment the effectiveness of pay in the fulfilment of their basic needs declines. Demands are raised for higher monetary benefits, either in the shape of increased pay or in the form of allowances and bonus, etc.

Besides adequacy, stability and regularity in payment are of vital importance to the wage earner. Since pay remains the principal source of their earnings, they expect its payment to be regular and stable. Irregularity in payment or even fluctuations in the amount disturb the family budgets of the wage and salary earners which causes not only economic hardships but also strained relations in the family. A worker spends roughly one third of his time at his work-place and out of the remaining two thirds of his time, he probably spends more than half in the family, from where he obtains the fulfilment of his social needs besides over coming the monotony or tedious tensions of the work place. Every individual worker tries to create a cordial and tension-free climate in his family.

The effectiveness of pay in the fulfilment of the basic needs of an individual depends not on the face value of his money, but on the purchasing power of his money, his real income. The real income in turn is influenced by the price-index or cost of living index.

Table 4.11. Strikes on higher pay and cost of living index

Period	*Percentage of strike on wage increase to total of economic strikes*	*Cost of living index*			*Average annual increase*
1964-67	32	118 170	—	1964 1967	13.0
1968-71	21	175 189	—	1968 1971	3.5
1972-75	47	204 327	—	1972 1975	30.7
1976-80	30	295 395	—	1976 1980	20.0
1981-85	38	429 607	—	1981 1985	35.6

Source: 1. Labour Directorate, Government of Orissa
2. Indian Labour Journal.

Over the last few decades there has been considerable increase in money earnings of workers. The average annual money earnings of workers increased from Rs. 1985 (1968) to Rs. 6026 (1978) and to Rs. 12,898 (1981). Real earnings during this same period also increased but at a rate much lower than that of money income. The cost of living index almost doubled between 1968 and 1980. It increased from 175 to 395. The average retail price of a kilogram of rice (Government fixed support price of common rice) which was Rs. 1.08 in 1968 increased to Rs. 2.24 in 1975 and 2.90 in 1988-89. This increase in price index acted as an instigating force behind the workers' demand for higher wages. Table 4.11 shows the linkage between strikes for higher pay and cost of living index.

The study reveals a positive linkage between cost of living index and strike activity on wage increase. During 1964-67, 32 per cent of the strikes on economic issues were based on demand for higher pay, and the cost of living index during this period increased by 52 points i.e. from 118 in 1964 to 170 in 1967. But during 1968-71 its proportion declined to 21 when cost of living index rose marginally, only by 14 points, i.e. from 175 in 1967 to 189 in 1971. Similarly, the period between 1972 and 1975, which witnessed a steep rise in the cost of living index i.e. from 189 in 1971 to 327 in 1975, also witnessed the highest proportion of strikes on wage demands. During this period 47 per cent of strikes on economic issues were demands for higher wages. Between 1981-85, strikes on demand of higher wage increased by 8 per cent in comparison with the period 1976-80 which establishes a close link with the cost of price index, which increased from 295 in 1976 to 429 in 1981.

Again, when strike activity on wage demand is compared with the retail price of the common variety of rice the study reveals a close relationship between strike activity on higher wage and the retail prices of rice.

During 1964-67, when 32 per cent of economic demands were based on higher wage, the price of common rice was Rs. 1.08 per kilogram. But during 1968-71, when the price of rice fell to Rs. 1.06 per kilogram demand for wage increase accounted for only 21 per cent of economic demands. Again in 1975 when the price of common rice rose to Rs. 2.24 demand for wage increase accounted for 40 per cent of the economic demands during 1972-75. Again in 1980 when the price of rice fell to Rs. 2.07, the percentage of strike on wage increase declined to 30 per cent. It also increased to 38 per cent during 1981-85, when the price of rice increased to 2.59 paise per kg. Table 4.12 shows the linkage between the price of common rice and strikes on higher wages.

Table 4.12. Strikes on higher pay and price of rice

Period	*Percentage of strikes on wage increase to strike on economic issues*	*Retail price of common rice. (Rs. per kg.)*
1964-67	32	1.08
1968-71	21	1.06
1972-75	47	2.24
1976-80	30	2.07
1981-85	38	2.59

Source: 1. Labour Directorate, Government of Orissa
2. Statistical Abstract of Orissa, Bureau of Economics and Statistics.

Table 4.13 shows that during the 60's when the cost of living index was roughly 143, about 41 per cent of economic demands were based on wage increase. Rice, being the staple food of people living in Orissa, its price greatly affects the cost of living index. The

Table 4.13. Strikes on higher pay demands and cost of living index, retail price of common rice during the 1960's and 1980's

Period	*Economic issues annual average*	*Wage increase annual average*	*Cost of living index*	*Retail price of common rice in (Rs.)*	*Percentage of strikes in wage increase to total of economic issues*
1960's	17	7	143	0.95	41
1970's	32	20	362	1.65	63
Total	25	5	—	—	57.8

retail price of common rice during this period was 0.95 paise per kilogram. But during the 1970's when cost of living index jumped from 143 to 362, and the cost of the common variety of rice rose from 0.95 paise per kilogram to Rs. 1.65 paise per kilogram, the proportion of wage increase to the total of economic demands rose accordingly. During the 1970's, roughly 63 per cent of economic demands were directly on wage demands.

Statistically also there was a positive correlation between the number of strikes and variables like cost of living index, daily average employment and average annual earnings. Necessary data showing co-efficient of correlation between these variables between 1971-85 are given below.

Table 4.14. The number of strikes, cost of living index, wholesale price, daily average employment and average annual earnings

Year	*No. of strikes*	*Cost of living index*	*Index of wholesale price*	*Daily average employment*	*Average annual money earning*
1971	27	189	105.6	74,798	3,040
1972	26	204	116.2	70,977	3,451
1973	63	223	139.7	71,983	4,842
1974	60	293	174.9	74,215	3,536
1975	34	327	173.0	73,696	3,566
1976	45	295	176.6	80,974	5,166
1977	65	322	185.6	78,483	5,970
1978	102	331	185.8	82,581	6,026
1979	95	349	217.6	85,416	7,228
1980	86	395	254.5	97,307	5,775
1981	87	429	—	1,36,130	12,898
1985	110	607	357.8	1,44,264	—

Source: Statistical Abstract of Orissa, Bureau of Economics and Statistics, Orissa.

Table 4.15 shows positive correlation between strikes and cost of living index. It is +0.54. This relationship becomes more positive when compared with the wholesale price index. Strike activity is positively related with average annual earning, but not so strongly as with the wholesale price index or cost of living index.

Table 4.15. Co-efficient of correlation between strikes and cost of living index, wholesale price index, average annual earnings per worker and daily average employment

Variables	*Co-efficient of correlation*
Cost of living index	+ 0.54
Whole price index	+ 0.71
Average annual earning per worker	+ 0.11
Daily average employment	+ 0.30

This statistical correlation between strikes and cost of living index and with average annual earnings of workers thus supports the findings of Vanderkamp, and others. Their studies have found a positive correlation between strike activity and the cost of living index. According to Vanderkamp, if workers are strongly influenced by changes in the cost of living but the firm's position is less directly affected, then substantial rises in the consumer price index will tend to increase strike activity.

This study, too, reveals a similar relationship between cost of living index and total strike activity. The findings go a little further and prove that during the period under observation, most of the strikes revolved round wage increase. The other notable feature of the analysis is that the positive correlation between strikes on wage increase and cost of living index is more stronger when compared with total strike activity. The co-efficient of correlation between total strikes and cost of living index is +0.5 whereas it is + 0.6 with strikes on wage increase. The co-relation co-efficient between total strikes and average annual earning of a worker is only +0.1 which is +0.4 when co-related with strikes on wage increase. Table 4.16 shows co-efficient correlation between strikes on wage increase and cost of price index average annual earnings of an industrial workers.

Table 4.16. Correlation Co-efficient between Strikes on Wage Increase and Cost of Price Index, Average Annual Earnings

Variables	*Co-efficient of correlation*
Cost of living index	+ 0.6
Average annual earning	+ 0.4

NON-IMPLEMENTATION OF WAGE BOARD RECOMMENDATIONS AND NON-PAYMENT OF WAGES

The next important wage issues are the non-payment of wages and non-implementation of Wage Board recommendations. During the period under study strike demands on non-payment of wages fluctuated from 20 per cent to 26 per cent of the total wage disputes, the average for the period came to 22 per cent. Strike demands on non-implementation of Wage Board decisions constituted very negligible percentages except between 1968-71 when it was roughly 34 per cent of the wage demands.

The payment of Wage Act of 1936 stipulates that the person responsible for the payment of wages shall fix the wage periods in respect of which wages shall be payable. Such period shall not exceed one month.

Sections 4 to 6 of the Act deals with the rules regarding the time of payment of wages.

(a) In a railway, factory, or industrial establishment in which less than 1000 persons are employed, wages must be paid before the expiry of the seventh day after the last day of the wage period in respect of which the wages are payable. In all other cases, wages must be paid before the expiry of the tenth day after the last day of the wage period.

(b) All payments must be made on a working day.

(c) All wages shall be paid in current coins or currency notes or in both.

The Act also imposes punishment on the employer who does not (i) fix the period for payment of wages or (ii) does not pay wages on a working day or (iii) does not pay wages in current coin or currency notes or (iv) does not record all fines realisations in a prescribed register.

Every employer who contravenes these provisions is liable to pay a fine extending upto Rs. 200.

The problem of non-payment or of irregular payment does not exist in organised sector, where trade unions are relatively strong and there is better enforcement of the provisions of the Act. The problem of non-payment including that of irregular payment lies mostly in unorganised sectors, which are covered under the Minimum Wages Act of 1948.

In Orissa the Minimum Wages Rules were framed in 1954, under which the State Government assumed power to bring any industry in the Schedule employment and fix and refix wages in these industries. Presently, Agriculture, Rice Mills, Flour Mills, Beedi and Tobacco, Municipality Construction Corporation, Public Motor Transport, Cinema, Printing Presses, Salt Manufacturing, Bamboo Cutting, Saw Mills, Private Road Transport, Shops and Commercial establishments, Oil Mills, Chemical Industries etc. are covered under the Minimum Wages Act.

The study discloses that on an average 12 per cent of the economic demands were based on non-payment of increased wages fixed either under the Minimum Wages Act or under the Wage Board recommendations.

Its proportion has varied from a minimum of 7 per cent during 1972-75 to a minimum of 10 per cent between 1986-89. The study further disclosed two interesting features:

1. Most of the strikes on non-payment of wages were confined to units covered under the Minimum Wages Act. For example during 1964-67, 9 out of the 10 strikes took place in establishments covered under the Minimum Wages Act. Similarly during 1976-80, out of 19 strikes 16 or roughly 84 per cent took place in establishments like printing presses, constructions, etc. which are covered under Scheduled employments.
2. The second interesting feature was the timing of such strike demands. Most of these strikes took place when either new establishments were brought under the purview of Minimum Wages Act or the existing wage rates were revised. The inclusion of several new establishments within the purview of the Act and revision of the existing new wage rates in 1976, led to roughly 18 per cent of strikes on this particular issues, as against only 7 per cent during 1972-75, when very few new establishments were brought under the purview of this Act.

The rule was revised on 26th December, 1975. Many new employments were brought under the purview of the Act and the minimum wage was fixed in these employments and revised in the existing employments. Further revision of minimum wages on 30.3.1982, 15.7.1986 and on 22.7.1987 has its impact on strikes relating to non-payment of wages. Between 1982-83, 22 per cent strikes were caused by this issue and during 1987-89, 18 per cent of strikes were declared on non-payment of wages.

This shows that a particular time period has also an influence on strike activity. When any provision is made by the legislature to provide benefits to workers and the management delays implementing the provisions, workers resort to strike. They also resort to strike to register their protests when they find the provisions not favourable to their interests.

The other important issue is the non-implementation of Wage Board recommendations. During the period under study except 1968- 71, a very negligible percentage of strikes were declared on non- implementation of Wage Board recommendations.

The first Central Wage Board was appointed for the cotton textile industry in March 1957 (second in 1964). Subsequently Wage Boards came to be set up for Sugar (1957 and 1965), Cement (1958 and 1964), Jute (1960) Tea Plantation (1961), Iron and Steel (1962), Coal Mining (1962), Non-journalists (1964), Heavy Chemicals and Fertilizers (1965), Leather and Leather Goods (1966), Electricity Undertakings (1966) and Road Transport Industries (1966).

Since 1957, 24 Wage Boards have been set up. The Wage Boards generally take 3 to 5 years for the submission of their reports. The unanimous recommendations are written down in the form of a report and submitted to the Government. The Government usually accepts the unanimous decisions, although it may modify any provision thereof. The report is sent to the concerned parties after getting the approval of the Government. The Government has no legal power to enforce the Board's recommendations. It tries to persuade the parties to narrow their differences and aim at unanimity.

This process itself becomes the cause of anxiety among the workers. There have been frequent outbursts of strikes on the issues involving implementation of Wage Board recommendations, grant of interim relief, appointment of Wage Board, etc.

In Orissa, most of the large industries like the Iron and Steel, Cotton Textile, Cement, Sugar, Electricity undertaking, Heavy Chemicals and Fertilizers were covered under Wage Boards. During the period under study roughly 6 per cent of the economic demands were on non-implementation of Wage Board recommendations. During (1968-71) out of 29 strikes on economic issues, 11 strikes were declared on this particular issue i.e. roughly 34 per cent of strikes were caused by the non-implementation of Wage Board recommendations.

During 1968-71 out of 11 strikes on non-implementation of Wage Board recommendations 4 occurred in engineering, 2 in textiles, 2 in cement industry, one in electricity generation and distribution, and the remaining two in non-manufacturing sectors, namely, working journalists and non-journalists year-wise would reveal that two such strikes occurred in 1968, one was declared by the workmen of "The Samaja" a local daily on account of the non-implementation of the recommendations of the Central Wage Board for non-journalists on 10th October, 1968. The other one was declared by the employees of the Newspaper establishments, The Samaja, The Kalinga, The Prajatantra, The Matrubhumi and Janasakti all located at Cuttack under the leadership of the Utkal Journalists' Association, All Orissa Newspapers Employees' Association and Press Workers' Union, demanding implementation of the recommendations of the Wage Board for working journalists and non-journalists on 23rd April 1968.

In 1970, one strike occurred in Indian Aluminium Co. Ltd. Hirakud demanding implementation of the final recommendation of the Central Wage Board for the Engineering Industry. On the same issue 3 strikes were declared in three different organisations— the Hirakud Industrial Works, the Re-rolling Mills, and the Aluminium Industries, all situated in Hirakud. Another engineering concern Kalinga Iron Works, Matkambeda (I.D.C.) also experienced a strike on the same issue. The workers of the Bhaskar Textiles, Jharsuguda, resorted to strike to give effect to the recommendations of the Second Cotton Textile Wage Board. The workers of the State Electricity Board also declared a strike demanding the implementation of the Central Wage Board's recommendations for electricity undertakings.

In 1971, the workers of the Bhaskar Textile Mills again resorted to strike on the same issue.

The above discussions clearly show that the recommendations of the Wage Boards inspired the workers to declare strikes in certain specific establishments during 1968-71, which constituted 34 per cent of the strikes on economic issues.

This shows that strikes on specific causes are influenced by a particular time period.

Bonus, an important economic issue in strike activity, is also influenced by specific time period. On an average 3 strikes per year took place on bonus demands, between 1964 and 80. Roughly 20 per cent of the economic demands were on bonus.

The enactment of the Bonus Act in 1965 which made provisions for payment of a minimum bonus of 4.33 per cent and a maximum of 20 per cent witnessed a series of strikes based on the bonus issue. For example, during 1964-67, roughly 23 per cent of economic demands were caused by bonus issues. Again in 1975, when the Bonus Act was amended making 8.33 per cent the minimum bonus, a series of strikes occurred demanding implementation of the provisions of the amended Act. Roughly 30 per cent of the economic demands were on bonus issues during 1976-80.

On the basis of the above mentioned analysis, one can conclude that legislative measures do influence strike activity. When a particular legislation giving some benefits is enacted, the period immediately following the enactment witnesses a spate of strike activity. As years pass by, things normalise, ultimately reducing strike activity.

On the whole, the analysis revealed that economic demands were decreasing over the decades and strikes on personnel issues were increasing.

This trend emerged because of the fact that economic issues like wage fixation, payment of wages, bonus and allowances are regulated by various legislative measures like the Minimum Wages Act of 1948, Payment of Wages Act 1936, Payment of Bonus Act 1965, Provident Funds Act of 1952. Besides legislative, non-legislative measures like active involvement of Government through Industrial Tribunals, constitution of Wage Boards for organised sector, etc. have also helped in reducing strike activity for fulfilment of the economic demands of workers. This, however, does not mean that no efforts have been made to regulate service conditions and other personnel problems with which industrial workers are faced frequently. A number of legislative measures have been enacted which aim at regulating the terms and conditions of employment. For example, the Industrial Employment (Standing Orders) Act, 1946, Factories Act, 1948, Shops and Commercial Establishment Act, 1952, aim at regulating the terms and conditions of employment and working conditions of industrial workers.

In spite of these legislative measures strikes on non- economic issues have increased at a rate faster than those on economic issues, during 1960's and 1970's. In comparison to 1970's, strikes on economic issues increased by more than 3 per cent between 1981-89 whereas strikes on non-economic issues decreased by 2 per cent. But among non-economic issues protest against disciplinary action and misbehaviour by the management increased at a faster rate during 1980's. A number of factors are responsible for this, the first and foremost being the changing structure of the industrial work force. An industrial worker of to-day is very different from his predecessor. He has now a personality of his own. He shares the benefits of a Welfare State. He enjoys a measure of social security; he feels secure in his employment as he is given statutory protection against retrenchment, lay off, and unjust disciplinary actions. But he is not free from worries about the future of his dependents, the employment situation in the country being difficult. The changing social and political climate in the country has its own effect on worker. There has developed a greater sense of equality among workers. In fact, workers are becoming conscious of the distinction between workers and other staff members. A worker to-day is politically more conscious than before. Because the worker has not yet reached a standard which he considers satisfactory his inclination would be primarily to struggle for his rights. Increase of strikes on economic issues during 1980's is due to the revision of minimum wages in certain scheduled employments in 1982, 1986, 1987 and because of sharp rise in the cost of price index.

Secondly, because of the increase in the degree of unionisation, the industrial workforce to-day is much more organised than it was two decades ago. The table below gives the degree of unionisation in Orissa since 1950.

Table 4.17. Growth of trade unions in Orissa since 1950

Year	*No. of Trade Unions*	*Index*	*Union Membership*	*Index*
1950	84	100	26,206	100
1960	107	127	58,157	222
1970	216	257	1,11,799	427
1980	671	799	3,21,411	1226
1987	892	1062	5,80,069	2213

Source: The Labour Directorate, Government of Orissa.

In 1950 there were 84 Unions with 26,206 members. But in 1980, the number of Unions increased by more than 7 times and the membership more than 10 times. But in 1987, the number of unions and membership increased by more than 10 and 22 times respectively. This shows that over the decades trade unions have acquired numerical strength and stabilised their position.

Thirdly, the various legislative measures and the various decisions of the Supreme Court have provided a sense of job security to industrial labour.

Fourthly, psychological reasons—as per Maslownian psychology once the physiological needs, need for security are met, an individual wants to fulfil other needs, like recognition, status a greater degree of personal freedom, etc. This is the reason why workers to-day demand for worker's participation in management and give emphasis on collective bargaining, etc. Once upon a time they were considered as purely the perogative of the management. But that is being eroded and has become a subject matter of negotiations.

Owing to the above mentioned reasons, strike activity is increasing at a faster rate on non-payment of increased wages and as a protest against disciplinary action and misbehaviour of management.

INFLUENCE OF PLANT SIZE ON THE NATURE OF STRIKE DEMAND

The analysis has shown that both small and large sized organisations are affected by strike activity. It is now proposed to examine the nature and pattern of strike activity in organisations of different sizes. Such a study will reveal that the nature of strike activity remains identical in both small and large sized organisations. Economic issues remain dominant in small as well as big organisations, followed by personnel issues. Necessary data showing the pattern of strike activity in small and big organisations are given in the table below:

Table 4.18. Influence of plant size on the nature of strike demands during 1978-80

Size of the Plant	*Nature of Demands*		
	Economic	*Personnel*	*Other Issues*
Upto 100	57 (53.7)	40 (37.7)	9 (8.4)
101-500	57 (51.3)	36 (32.4)	18 (16.2)
501-1000	17 (50.0)	10 (29.4)	7 (20.5)
1000 and above	16 (50.0)	10 (30.3)	7 (21.1)
Total	147	96	41

Source: Labour Directorate, Government of Orissa
Percentage has been calculated by the researcher.

N. B.: Figures in bracket indicate percentage.

Thus, in small sized organisations, (upto 100) out of 106, 57 strikes (roughly 54 per cent) took place on economic reasons, 40 (38%) on personnel issues and 9 (8%) on other issues. In big organisations (1000 and above) out of 33 strikes 16 (50%) of the strikes were caused by economic issues, 10 (30%) on personnel issues and 7 (21%) on other issues.

But how the workers respond to the strike call in large and small sized organisations is an important aspect of the analysis. Incidence of strike is not an alarming problem. In, Industrial democracy, conflicts do exist if neither party is dominating. But is important to consider how the conflict gets resolved and how the workers support the strike.

IMPACT OF PLANT SIZE ON STRIKERS' PARTICIPATION RATE

Worker's response to strike differs according to the size of the organisation. Worker's participation rate is usually high in small sized organisation and low in large sized organisations. The classification of workers' participation rate in strike activity according to size of organisations given in the table 4.19 shows that in small organisation employing upto 100 workers, roughly 62 per cent of the strike was supported by more than 75 per cent of the work-force. In large organisations employing more than 1000 workers only 33 per cent of strikes was supported by such a high proportion of the work force.

Table 4.19. Rate of participation in strike activity according to size of organisations

Size of the Plant	*Percentage of worker involvement*					
	Below 10%	*10 to 20%*	*21 to 50%*	*51 to 75%*	*76 and above*	*total strike*
Upto 100	—	2 (1.8)	18 (16.9)	20 (18.9)	66 (62.3)	106
101-500	12 (10.8)	7 (6.3)	22 (19.8)	12 (10.8)	58 (52.3)	111
501-1000	5 (14.8)	6 (17.7)	2 (5.08)	3 (8.8)	18 (52.9)	34
1000 and above	5 (15.2)	7 (21.2))	6 (18.2)	4 (12.1)	11 (33.3)	33

Source: Labour Directorate, Government of Orissa
Percentage has been calculated by the researcher.

N. B.: Figures in bracket indicate percentage.

In organisation employing 101 to 1000 workers 52 per cent of the strikes was supported by 75 per cent of workers. In large sized organisations employing more than 1000 workers about 36 per cent of strikes was supported by 20 per cent of workers. But in small sized organisations employing upto 100 persons, only 2 per cent of strikes were supported by 20 per cent of workers. On the basis of above finding, one may conclude that the possibility of having mass supported strikes are greater in small sized organisations and less in large organisations.

For example, in organisations-employing 501 to 1000 workers only 34 per cent of strikes were supported by more than 76 per cent of the work force and 43 per cent of the strikes had the support of more than 50 per cent of the work force. In organisations employing more than 1000 workers only 30 per cent of strikes had the support of more than 76 per cent of the work force and about 15 per cent of the strikes had the support of less than 10 per cent of the work force.

From the above analysis one may derive the following conclusions:

(1) In small units most of the strikes are supported by the majority i.e. more than 50 per cent of the work force, and quite a large number of such strikes enjoy the support of almost all the workers. Because of their smallness, there is a greater degree of cohesiveness among workers of small units.

(2) However, in large units relatively small numbers of strikes are supported by the majority of workers.

(3) A plant-wise strike involving cent per cent participation is possible in small units but not in large units.

Table 4.20. Rate of Participation of Workers in Strikes Classified by Causes

Percentage of workers involved to total work force of the organisation	*Economic issues*	*Personnel*	*Other issues*
Below 10%	7 (4.7)	11 (11.4)	4 (9.7)
10-20%	8 (5.4)	10 (10.4)	4 (9.7)
21-50%	21 (14.2)	16 (16.6)	11 (26.8)
51-75%	19 (12.8)	17 (17.7)	2 (4.8)
76-100%	92 (62.5)	42 (43.7)	20 (48.7)

Source: Labour Directorate, Government of Orissa
N. B.: Figures in bracket indicate percentage.

Participation of workers in strike action shows the real importance of the strike demand. Involvement of workers in strikes on different demands like economic, personnel and other issues would reveal the real interest of working in strikes. The table below summarises the rate of participation of workers in strikes classified by causes during 1978-80.

Table 4.20 explains that during 1978-80 out of 147 strikes declared on economic issues, 92 strikes were supported by (76-100 per cent) of workers employed in the concerned organisations. About 63 per cent of the strikes on economic issues were supported by more than 76 per cent of the workers. Again, more than 75 per cent of the strikes were supported by more than 50 per cent of the workers. Less than 5 per cent of the strikes on economic issues were supported by less than 10 per cent of the workers.

Strikes declared on personnel issues enjoyed relatively less support from workers in comparison to strikes on personnel issues were supported by more than 76 per cent of the work force. Strikes have been increasing in numbers during recent years but the participation rate is not alarming.

The rate of participation depends on two factors: faith in the leadership and gravity of the problem. As economic problem is a major problem for the worker; he supports the strike on economic issue giving less thought to the after effect of strike. But when other issues are involved they have to give a second thought to it because they fear the post-effects of the strike.

Workers are also motivated by the leaders who assure them economic benefits through strike action. But it is difficult to motivate the workers when they themselves do not realise the importance of the problem. Sometimes the workers supports strike if they have a strong faith in the leadership and expect better results. Generally the strike call is given by the Union leader. In Orissa majority of the strikes have been declared by Unions. Unions being influenced by political parties, sometimes strikes are declared with political objectives. To give a strike call is not difficult but to get the support of the majority of workers is a vital issue. The majority of Indian industrial workers are illiterate but not ignorant of their rights and duties. So also the workers of Orissa. Some of them can be motivated but to motivate the bulk of the workers is not an easy task. Strike can be called only as a last resort to impose a demand on an unwilling employer. It might bring success to workers or it might end in failure. Thus, the wo:kers do not blindly support strikes. Only when they develop faith in the unity of workers will they be willing go on strike.

Where a large number of workers work together, there is every possibility of differences of opinion among them. They belong to different groups and from different unions. Unions become rival to each other. Inter and intra union rivalries divide the workers as well as the leaders of the organisation. So in large plants, greater participation is a rare phenomenon.

The analysis on the foregoing pages have proved that the nature of demand and the size of the organisation greatly influence the participation rate. It is now proposed to examine the participation rate demand-wise and according to size of the organisation.

Data analysed in the following tables shows the rate of participation in different types of organisation on different issues.

Table 4.21. Rate of participation in small sized organisation (upto 100)

Nature of demands	*Size of the plant (upto 100)*					
	Percentage of workers involved to total work force of the organisation					
	Below 10%	*11-20%*	*21-50%*	*51-75%*	*76-100%*	*Total*
Economic	—	1 (1.7)	5 (8.8)	9 (16.0)	41 (73.2)	56
Personnel	—	1 (2.5)	8 (20.0)	10 (25.0)	21 (52.5)	40
Other issues	—	—	5 (50.0)	1 (10.0)	4 (40.0)	10
Total	—	2	18	20	66	106

Source: Labour Directorate, Government of Orissa
N. B.: Figures in bracket indicate percentage.

The table above explains in small sized organisations more than 73 per cent of strikes declared on economic issues got the support of more than 76 per cent workers of the concerned organisations. About 90 per cent of the strikes were supported by more than 50 per cent of the workers.

Roughly 53 per cent of the strikes declared on personnel issues were supported by more than 76 per cent workers of the concerned organisations. About 90 per cent of the strikes were supported by more than 50 per cent of the workers.

Roughly 53 per cent of the strikes declared on personnel issues were supported by more than 76 per cent of the workers and more than 77 per cent of strikes were supported by more than 50 per cent workers. Out of 100, only 2 strikes were supported by below 20 per cent of workers.

Table 4.22. Rate of participation in organisations having (101- 500) employees

Nature of demands	*Percentage of workers involved to total work force of the concerned organisation*					
	Below 10%	*11-20 %*	*21-50 %*	*51-75 %*	*76-100 %*	*Total No. of strikes*
Economic	3 (5.2)	3 (5.2)	10 (17.5)	7 (12.2)	34 (59.6)	57
Personnel	7 (19.9)	2 (5.6)	7 (19.4)	5 (13.9)	15 (41.7)	36
Other issues	2 (11.1)	2 (11.1)	5 (27.7)	—	9 (50.0)	18

Source: Labour Directorate, Government of Orissa
Percentage has been calculated by the researcher.

N. B.: Figures in bracket indicate percentage.

Table 4.23. Rate of participation of different demands in organisations employing (501-1000) employees

	Percentage of workers involved to total work force of the concerned organisation					
	Below 10%	*11-20%*	*21-50%*	*51-75%*	*76-100%*	*Total No. of strikes*
Economic	2 (11.7)	3 (17.6)	1 (5.8)	2 (11.7)	9 (52.9)	17
Personnel	2 (20.0)	2 (20.0)	1 (10.0)	1 (10.0)	4 (40.0)	10
Other issues	1 (14.3)	1 (14.3)	—	—	5 (71.4)	7

Source: Labour Directorate, Government of Orissa

N. B.: Figures in bracket indicate percentage.

Only 40 per cent strikes declared on other issues were supported by a majority of workers and 50 per cent of the strikes were participated in by below 50 per cent of workers.

This analysis shows that mass supported strikes were more on economic issues. About 60 per cent of the strikes on economic issues were supported by more than 76 per cent of workers. Only 5 per cent of the strikes were supported by lowest number of workers. More than 70 per cent of strikes were declared with 50 per cent support on economic issues.

Roughly 42 per cent of the strikes on personnel issues had mass support. Roughly 20 per cent of the strikes got the support of below 10 per cent of the workers. Out of 100,50 strikes on other issues were supported by majority workers.

The above analysis shows that out of 100 strikes declared on economic issues, 53 strikes got majority support. But on personnel issues only 40 per cent of strikes were supported by a majority of workers. But strikes declared with the support of a low percentage of workers were not rare. Out of 100 strikes 20 strikes were declared with the support of 10 per cent of workers.

Table 4.24. Rate of Participation in Strikes Declared on Different Demands in Large Sized Organisations (Employing More than 1000 Employees)

	Percentage of workers involved to total work force of the organisation					
	Below 10%	*11-20%*	*21-50%*	*51-75%*	*76-100%*	*Total No. of strikes*
Economic	1 (7.1)	—	5 (35.7)	1 (7.1)	7 (50.0)	14
Personnel	2 (20.0)	5 (50.0)	—	1 (10.0)	2 (20.0)	10
Other issues	1 (14.3)	1 (14.3)	1 (14.3)	2 (28.6)	2 (28.6)	7

N. B.: Figures in bracket indicate percentage.

In large sized organisations 50% of the strikes declared on economic issues were supported by cent per cent workers. On personnel issues only 20 per cent strikes were declared with a majority support. An interesting feature of this analysis is that 70 per cent of strikes were declared with below 50 per cent workers' support and only 30 per cent strikes had not support of more than 50 per cent workers.

On the whole, the analysis shows that most of the strikes with more than 76 per cent participation rate were economic strikes. Secondly most of the strikes with less than 20 per cent participation rate were on personnel issues. For example out of the total of 153 strikes, where participation rate was more than 75 per cent, 65 per cent of strikes were declared on economic issues, 27 per cent on personnel issues and 8 per cent on other issues. Again out of 44 strikes, where participation rate was of less than 20 per cent 50 per cent of strikes were declared on personnel issues, 34 per cent on economic issues and 16 per cent on other issues.

On the basis of above analysis one may conclude that strikes on economic issues attract more participants than other strikes declared on personnel and other issues.

SUMMARY

The following are the main themes of this chapter:

1. Strike is a complex phenomenon and is caused by various factors.
2. Both economic and non-economic issues may lead to strike.
3. In Orissa, economic, personnel and charter of demands are the three important causative factors of strike activity.
4. Economic strikes are mostly influenced by the need of the particular time period.
5. Strikes on personnel issues particularly on protest against disciplinary action and misbehaviour of management are increasing at a faster rate than other strikes during the recent period.
6. Majority of economic strikes are participated by more than 76 per cent of workers.

5

OTHER FEATURES OF STRIKE ACTIVITY

INTER - INDUSTRY PROPENSITY TO STRIKE

To understand the impact of industrial organisation, work force, technology, style of work and concentration of industries in industrial centres on industrial conflict, an attempt is made to find out variations in strike activity among industries. It has been stated in Chapter 2 that strike activity varies considerably among industries.

Industry-wise distribution of strikes in Orissa reveals that Iron and Steel, Textile, Paper and Paper Products, Electricity, Transport, Aluminium, Chemical, Basic Metals and Ferro Alloys, Ceramic, Machine and Machine Products, etc. predominated strike statistics between 1971-80 and 1981-89. Industrial composition of strike aggregates shows that out of a total of 603 strikes between 1971-80, 353 strikes occured in these industries. During 1980's also out of 658 strikes, 461 strikes occurred in these industries.

Among these industries, iron and steel alone accounted for roughly 14 per cent of strikes between 1971-80. The analysis further shows that some industries like sugar, glass-making, beedi and tobacco, etc. were less affected by strikes. The following table gives the percentage distribution of strikes among different industries from 1971 to 80 and 1981 to 89.

Table 5.1. Percentage Distribution of Strikes Among Industries

Industry	*Percentage*
Iron and Steel	13.9
Paper and Paper Products	11.1
Textile	8.1
Transport	7.7
Machine and Machine Products	6.1
Electricity	4.1
Basic Metal and Ferro-Alloys	2.4
Ceramic and Refractories	2.1
Chemical and Chemical Products	1.4
Rice and Flour Mills	1.2
Aluminium	1.1
Beedi and Tobacco	0.3
Cement	0.3
Electrical Machine Equipment	0.1
Sugar	0.1
Glass	0.1
Other Industries	37.6

Source: The Labour Directorate, Government of Orissa.

The table 5.1 thus shows that out of them the first eight industries accounted for more than 55 per cent of strikes from 1971 to 80 and occupied the first eight ranks on the basis of frequency of strikes.

Between 1981-89, there is change in ranking position of industries when compared with 1971-80. During 1981-89 the first eight industries accounted for more than 63 per cent of strikes. Table 5.2 shows the percentage distribution of strikes among industries between 1981-89.

Tables 5.3 and 5.4 give the relative ranks of these industries on the basis of frequency of strikes and man-days lost during 1971-80 and 1971-89.

Table 5.2. Percentage Distribution of Strikes Among Industries

Industry	*Percentage*
Iron and Steel	12.4
Machine and Machine Products	10.6
Textile	8.8
Chemical and Chemical Products	7.9
Aluminium	6.9
Metal and Metal Products	6.8
Electricity	5.4
Transport	4.6
Paper and Paper Products	4.6
Ceramic and Refractories	3.1
Cement	2.9
Electrical Machine Equipment	2.7
Rice and Flour Mills	0.9
Sugar	0.1
Glass	—
Beedi and Tobacco	—
Other Industries	23.4

Source: The Labour Directorate, Government of Orissa.

Table 5.3. Relative Ranking of Different Industries on the Basis of Strike Frequency and Man-days lost

Industry	*Total No. of Strikes*	*Ranking*	*Total No. of Man-days lost*	*Ranking*
Iron and Steel	84	1st	64,397	5th
Paper and Paper Products	67	2nd	66,705	4th
Textile	49	3rd	1,00,044	2nd
Transport	47	4th	55,235	6th
Machine and Machine Products	37	5th	73,602	3rd

Industry	*Total No. of Strikes*	*Ranking*	*Total No. of Man-days lost*	*Ranking*
Electricity	25	6th	2,24,399	1st
Basic Metal and Ferro-Alloys	16	7th	44,295	7th
Ceramic and Refractories	15	8th	41,071	8th
Chemical and Chemical Products	13	9th	17,912	9th
Rice and Flour Mills	9	10th	6,310	11th
Aluminium	7	11th	2,854	13th
Beedi and Tobacco	2	12th	463	16th
Cement		12th	5,395	12th
Electrical Machine Equipment	1	13th	1,000	15th
Sugar	1	13th	1,625	14th
Glass	1	13th	10,276	10th
Other Industries	227	—	8,21,303	—

Source: The Labour Directorate, Government of Orissa.

When the ranks of different industries were ascertained on the basis of man-days lost, almost a different picture emerged. During 1971-80, Iron and Steel, Paper and Paper Products and Textile, which occupied first three ranks on the basis of number of strikes, stepped to second, fourth and fifth position respectively, on the basis of man-days lost. Machine making industry which had 6th place in frequency ranking moved to Ist position in terms of man-days lost. Textile occupied 2nd and 3rd place in rank order of strike frequency and man-days lost respectively. However, these industries contributed the major percentage of strike statistics in absolute number and also in man-days lost. Between 1971-89 Iron and Steel, Textile, Machine and Machine Products which occupied first three ranks on the basis of number or strikes stepped to fourth, second and fifth position respectively on the basis of man-days lost.

Spearmen's rank correlation co-efficients were calculated to ascertain how closely the ranking of industry resembled in ranks between strike frequency and man-days lost.

Table 5.4. Relative Ranking of Different Industries between 1971-89

Industry	*Total No.*	*Ranking*	*Total No. of Man-days lost*	*Ranking*
Iron and Steel	170	1st	2,75,847	4th
Textile	112	2nd	3,84,399	2nd
Machine and Machine Products	107	3rd	1,80,844	5th
Paper and Paper Products	94	4th	4,81,946	1st
Chemical and Chemical Products	70	5th	87,746	8th
Metal Products and Ferro-Alloys	63	6th	70,417	10th
Transport	62	7th	1,11,484	7th
Electricity	60	8th	3,37,212	3rd
Aluminium	54	9th	1,45,358	6th
Ceramic and Refractories	37	10th	83,277	9th
Cement	21	11th	38,957	11th
Electrical Machine Equipment	19	12th	29,351	12th
Rice and Flour Mills	16	13th	6,835	14th
Sugar	1	14th	2,442	15th
Beedi and Tobacco	—	15th	463	16th
Glass		15th	12,426	13th
Miscellaneous	387	—	15,15,665	—

Source: The Labour Directorate, Government of Orissa.

Spearmen's rank correlation co-efficient is defined as :

$$r_k = 1 - \frac{6\,D^2}{N\,(N^2-1)} \quad \text{or}$$

$$\frac{1 - 6\left\{D^2 + \frac{1}{12}(m^3 - m)\right\}}{N^3 - N}$$

where r_k denotes rank co-efficient of correlation between number of strikes and man-days lost. D refers to the difference of ranks between paired items in two series. N represents number of paired items = 10. m refers to the number of times an item repeated. Hence m = 2

$$r_k = \frac{1 - 6\left\{D^2 + \frac{1}{12}(m^3 - m)\right\}}{N^3 - N}$$

$$= \frac{1 - \left\{81.5 + \frac{1}{12}(8-2)\right\}}{10^3 - 10}$$

$$= \frac{1 - 6\,(81.5 + 1/2)}{990}$$

$$= \frac{1 - 6\,(82)}{990}$$

$$= \frac{1 - 492}{990}$$

$$= 1 - 0.49 = +\ 0.5$$

$$r_k = +0.5$$

r_k being + 0.5 there exists positive rank correlation between strike frequency and man-days lost.

It is explained by the above findings that strikes were evenly distributed among industries. The most affected industries also vary in their position in ranking order of strike frequency and man-days lost. Their position may also change in different periods of analysis. However, these industries would remain as the most strike affected industries in terms of man-days lost and strike frequency.

Among these industries, all the industries were not equally strike prone or had the same propensity to strike. To find out the propensity to strike and nature of strike proneness, ten industries were selected from the ranking order given in table 5.5.

STRIKE PRONENESS

The table below shows the strike proneness of 10 most affected industries.

Table 5.5. Strike Proneness of 10 most affected Industries

Industry	*Percentage of Industrial Workers*	*Percentage of Workers Involved*	*Strike Prone Ratio*
Iron and Steel	27.5	10.06	0.36
Paper and Paper Products	8.4	10.6	1.26
Textile	9.05	11.2	1.23
Transport	2.1	6.69	3.10
Machine and Machine Products	2.81	10.6	3.70
Electricity	2.46	17.2	6.90
Ceramic and Refractories	7.3	5.8	0.79
Basic Metals and Ferro-Alloys	31.1	1.16	0.03
Chemical and Chemical Products	2.85	2.04	0.70
Rice and Flour Mills	4.1	3.26	0.79

Source: (i) The Labour Directorate, Government of Orissa.
(ii) Strike-prone ratio has been calculated according to above formula.

If the percentage of strikers in an industry is divided by the percentage of workers engaged in that industry, a ratio is obtained which signify the "Strike Proneness" of workers in that industry. The "Strike Propensity Ratio" shows only the extent to which workers in one industry are involved in strikes.

Table 5.5 disclosed that among the 10 most affected industries, electricity, transport, machine and machine products were highly strike-prone. Ceramic, basic metals, chemicals and rice and flour mills had low propensity to strike. Paper and paper products, textile showed low propensity to strike in comparison to electricity, transport and machine products. The notable feature of this analysis was that iron and steel which occupied first position in strike frequency ranking, showed very low propensity to strike i.e. 0.36. Except basic metal, iron and steel showed lowest propensity to strike in comparison to all other industries in the group.

For inter-industry comparison of strike proneness, Clark Kerr and Abraham Siegel in their study "The Inter-Industry Propensity to Strike—An International Comparison" classified industries as follows:

High	:	Man-days lost rank substantially above employment rank.
Medium-high	:	Man-days lost rank significantly above employment rank.
Medium	:	Man-days lost roughly proportionate to employment ranking.
Medium-low	:	Man-days lost rank significantly below employment ranking.
Low	:	Man-days lost rank substantially below employment ranking.

Table below shows the inter-industry comparison of strike-proneness in Orissa.

Table 5.6. Inter-industry Comparison of Strike-Proneness

Sl. No.	*Industry*	*Percentage of employment to total employment*	*Percentage of man-days lost to total man-days lost*
1.	Iron and Steel	27.5	4.1
2.	Paper and Paper Products	8.4	4.3
3.	Textile	9.05	6.5
4.	Transport	2.1	3.5
5.	Machine and Machine Products	2.8	4.7
6.	Electricity	2.46	14.6

7.	Ceramic and Refractories	7.3	2.8
8.	Basic Metals and Ferro-alloys	31.1	2.6
9.	Chemical and chemical products	2.85	1.16
10.	Rice and Flour Mills	0.79	0.41

Source: The Labour Directorate, government of Orissa.

On the basis of data analysed in table 5.4 and applying Kerr Siegel classification, the ten industries selected for inter- industry comparison of strike-proneness in Orissa may be grouped as follows:

Table 5.7. General Patterns of Strike

Propensity to Strike	*Industry*
High	Electricity
Medium High	Transport, Machine and Machine Products
Medium	Chemical, Rice and Flour Mills
Medium Low	Textile
Low	Iron and Steel, Basic Metal and Ferro-Alloys

This analysis again proves that electricity, transport, machine making were highly strike prone and iron and steel, basic metals etc. were low strike prone industries.

It is difficult to offer any explanation for the high strike propensity of electricity, transport and low propensity of iron and steel. Kerr-Siegel logic that the industries which were isolated would show higher strike propensities that industries whose workers were integrated into the rest of the society couldn't be applied to electricity, transport for high strike propensity or iron and steel industries for low strike propensity.

The authors advanced in the same article an alternative hypothesis for inter-industry strike differentials: the character of the job and the worker. According to the hypothesis, industries involving hard dirty work seemed to attract "tough, in constant combative and virile workers", who apparently took part in strikes as a way of expressing their manliness, or perhaps just because hard men did bold deeds. Industries with easy, pleasant job tasks on the other hand attracted a more submissive type of men who will abhor strikes. This hypothesis was also not appropriate for the present analysis because of character of job was not much different in iron and steel and electricity, especially generation of electricity.

In this respect, Edward Shorter and Charles Tilly's thesis holds good in Orissa, that "neither industrial organisation nor technology nor style of work nor any other variables make sense of the rank ordering strike propensities".

DURATION OF STRIKES

Workers resort to strike to press their demand on an unwilling employer. Strike call is given either by union or by the work-groups. To give a strike call is not important, the staying capacity of the strikers on strike determines the strength of the union and the strikers. Sometimes management ignores the strikers and set counter acting forces to supress them. Managerial response to the strike call depends on factors like strength of strikers in respect of their membership, financial position of strikers, nature of demand, business cycles and the possibility of replacing strikers with non-strikers and Government's reaction to strike.

The average duration of strike is a measure of the time an average striker spends on strike, i.e. the days lost per striker. It is obtained by dividing the number of working days lost by the number of workers involved for a particular year. The formula is:

$$\text{Average Duration } \frac{\text{Man–days lost (MD)}}{\text{Workers Involved (WI)}}$$

$$MD = NS \times \frac{WI}{NS} \times \frac{MD}{WI} \text{ (Number of Strikes)}$$

$$MD = NS \times \frac{WI}{NS} \times \frac{MD}{WI}$$

= Number of Strike x Average size x Average duration

The average duration of strike between 1966 and 1980 is given in Table 5.7.

Table 5.7. Average Duration of Strikes between 1966-89

Period	*Average Duration*
1966-70	15.7
1971-75	15.4
1976-80	8.1
1981-89	6.6

Source: The Labour Directorate, Government of Orissa..
N. B. The figures are calculated by the Researcher applying the above formula.

This table shows that the annual average duration of strike activity during 1966-70 was 15.7 days which decreased to 15.4 days during 1971-75. During the last part of 1970's it further declined to 8.1 striker days. During 1981-89, the average duration decreased to 6.6 days.

Prof. A.M. Ross has made some interesting international comparisons of duration of strikes. His study reveals that in most countries the average duration of strike has gone down over a period of time except U.S.A. where it remained static 14.6 days.

Generally shorter duration means that union leadership is stronger, management is constructive and collective bargaining and industrial conciliation are well established.

According to Sheila Hopkins there is some tendency for the duration of stoppages to vary inversely with industrial activity for either employer and/or employed to be more stubborn in a depression and more conciliatory when industry is prospering. This inverse relationship of employment and duration is less clearly marked than the relationship between employment and frequency. According to her study duration vary with the phases of trade cycle.

An attempt has been made on the basis of available data to examine if any relationship exists between the average duration and unemployment on the one hand and between average duration and average annual earnings of industrial workers on the other

The table below shows the relationship between average duration of strike and unemployment in Orissa during 1971-75 and 1976-80, and 1981-89.

Table 5.8. Average duration of strikes and unemployment

Period	*Average duration*	*Index*	*Unemploy-ment (Annual) Average number*	*Index*
1971-75	15.4	100	2,91,414	100
1976-80	8.1	53	3,96,100	136
1981-89	6.6	43	4,94,892	170

Source: The Labour Directorate, Government of Orissa.
Statistical Abstract of Orissa, 1979 published by Bureau of Statistics.
Index number calculated by the Researcher.

This analysis shows that when the rate of un-employment increased by 36 per cent average duration of strike decreased by 47 per cent i.e. from 15.1 days to 8.1 days, when it further increased by 70 per cent average duration decreased by 57 per cent i.e. from 15.1 days to 6.6 days. This establishes some relationship and explains that when alternative employment is less, worker becomes more conciliatory.

Again during periods of economic prosperity, the preparedness of Unions to accept or initiate strikes improves owing to improvement in the financial position of Unions. But workers do not favour prolonged strike during such period, to avoid any monetary loss arising out of prolonged strike. On the other hand, during such periods the employers earn better profits, hence they are also not in a mood to allow the workers to continue on strike. Thus during prosperity both the parties become conciliatory resulting in decline in average duration of strike. The table below shows the relationship between average annual earnings of industrial workers and average duration during 1971-75 and 1976-80 and 1981-89.

Table 5.9. Average Annual Earning of Industrial Workers and Average Duration of Strikes 1971-89

Period	*Average Annual earnings*	*Index*	*Average Duration*	*Index*
1971-75	3,687	100	15.4	100
1976-80	6,146	166	8.1	53
1981-89	12,898	350	6.6	43

Source: The Labour Directorate, Government of Orissa.
Index number has been calculated by the Researcher.

This analysis shows that when average annual earning of an industrial worker increases average duration of strike decreases. During 1971-75 average annual earning was Rs. 3687 which increased to 6146 during 1976-80 and it further increased to 12898 during 1981-89. Average duration of strike was 15.4 days during 1971-75 which decreased to 8.1 days during 1976-80 and 6.6 between 1981-89. When average annual earnings increased by 66 per cent, average duration decreased by 53 per cent. Further increase of average annual earnings resulted in decrease of average duration by 57 per cent. This shows that prosperity makes both the parties more conciliatory, resulting in decline in average duration of strikes.

LENGTH OF STRIKES

Workers' decision to declare a strike is influenced by many factors like finance, public reaction towards strike, leadership expectancy of the result, staying capacity of the workers, etc. Employers also deal with the workers taking many factors into consideration during a strike period. Capacity of the leaders to unite workers, justifiability of the demand, financial position of the union, unity among the workers, whether the strike is legal or illegal and what would be the public reaction.

In previous section of this chapter the average duration of strike in Orissa was analysed and it was found that gradually the average duration of strike in Orissa was coming down. In this section, an attempt has been made to analyse the length of strike. Length of strike refers to the number of days for which a strike continues. Length of stoppage is a useful index of the severity of a strike.

A study of length of strike in Orissa reveals that roughly one third of strikes during 1966-80, lasted for less than a day and another 32 per cent lasted for less than 5 days. This means that roughly two third of strikes, were settled in less than 5 days. Very few strikes, less than 13 per cent continued for more than three weeks. The Table 5.10 give the percentage distribution of strikes on the basis of length of strikes.

Periodic analysis shows that like average duration, the length of strike was also gradually declining. During the later part of sixties (1966-70) only 7 per cent of strikes could be settled on the same day which increased to 42 per cent during the later part of seventies (1976-80). Similarly the proportion of strikes lasting for more than three weeks also registered a sharp decline. During 1966-70, roughly 15 per cent of strikes lasted for more than 3 weeks, which declined to 11 per cent during 1976- 80. During 1980's, also the same trend continued roughly 60 per cent of strikes were settled within 5 days and about 12 per cent strikes lasted for more than 3 weeks.

The possible explanations for high percentage of strikes continuing upto 5 days and low percentage of strikes continuing more than 3 weeks are:

Table 5.10. Percentage Distribution of Strikes on the Basis of Length during 1966-89

Period	*Total no. of strikes*	*Less than a day*	*1-5 day*	*5-10 days*	*10-20 days*	*20-30 days*	*30 days and above*
1966-70	125	7.2	47.2	12.8	17.6	6.4	8.8
1971-75	219	30.9	35.2	12.3	7.6	3.3	10.4
1976-80	393	41.7	25.1	13.9	7.3	6.8	4.8
1981-85	371	28.3	26.1	15.6	11.05	4.04	4.5
1986-89	286	15.7	43.3	18.1	12.9	4.5	8.3
	1385		31.8	11.9	9.2	5.7	7.1

***Source*: The Labour Directorate, Government of Orissa..**

(i) It has been discussed in chapter III that in Orissa the conciliation machinery is playing an affective role in settling maximum number of disputes. In section V of this chapter, it has been analysed that roughly 70 per cent of the strikes were resolved by the intervention of the conciliation machinery.

The Industrial Disputes Act of 1947, provides that in public utility services, it is a statutory obligation on the part of the conciliation officer to hold conciliation proceedings where a notice of strike or lock-out is given under Section 22. In non- public utility services it is optional and he may hold conciliation proceedings. Under section 12 of the Act, the conciliation officer must submit the report within 14 days of the commencement of conciliation proceeding or within shorter period as may be fixed by the appropriate government and the time may be estimated by such period as may be agreed upon in writing by all parties to the dispute.

The present analysis discloses that more than 85 per cent of strikes was resolved within three weeks. One third of the total strikes were resolved within a day and two third took less than 5 days for settlement. This proves that the legislative provisions and active intervention of conciliation machinery help in settling maximum number of strikes within a short period.

(ii) Secondly, the nature of demand, size of the organisation, rate of participation in strikes, business conditions, unionisation have a combined influence on the attitude of management as well as labour to become conciliatory in reducing the number of prolonged strikes.

It has been discussed in chapter Vth that in Orissa economic issues was the main causes of strikes and the next important issue was personnel. Economic objective being the basic objective of all the workers majority of strikes were mass supported strikes. Neither workers nor management could ignore their economic interest. Keeping the business prospectives in view management cannot allow the mass supported strikes to continue for a longer period. The workers also cannot afford to bear economic loss. So both the parties have to reconcile and to settle the matter as per the provisions of the economic legislations like Minimum Wages Act,

1948, Payment of Wages Act, 1936 and Payment of Bonus Act, 1965. Like economic interest, employment security, promotion, transfer etc. also play a vital role to raise the status of a worker. Both the workers of large and small sized organisations have to take a cautious approach towards the strikes declared on personnel issues. The management also cannot ignore the worker's genuine demands on personnel issues because job conditions are regulated through legislative provisions and can be challenged in the court of law. Thus, majority of the strikes on economic and personnel issues were resolved within 5 days. The above explanations are supported by the data given in the table below:

Table 5.11. Percentage Distribution of Strikes on Different Issues according to their Length from 1971 to 1980

Issues	*Less than a day*	*1-5 days*	*5-10 days*	*10-20 days*	*20-30 days*	*30 days and above*
Economic	36.3	31.6	13.7	6.8	5.3	5.9
Personnel	38.7	25.0	15.8	10.7	5.6	3.5
Other Issues	38.6	26.1	19.3	15.9	5.6	5.6

Source: The Labour Directorate, Government of Orissa.

The above table discloses that from 1971 to 1980 out of 100 strikes on economic issues, 36 strikes were terminated within a day and 68 strikes continued upto 5 days and only 11 strikes took more than three weeks for settlement. Further the analysis shows that majority of strikes on personnel issues took 1-5 days and very few continued beyond three weeks. Roughly 39 strikes were settled within a day and more than 60 per cent of strikes resolved within 5 days. This shows that majority of strikes on economic and personnel issues are resolved in less than 5 days.

Further analysis shows that majority of strikes on economic and personnel issues were supported by more than 50 per cent workers. Maximum number of mass supported strikes were terminated within 5 days. The table below shows the percentage distribution of strikes on different issues according to their length and rate of participation between 1978 and 1980.

Table 5.12. Percentage Distribution of Strikes on Different Issues Resolved within 5 days According to Rate of Participation

Issue		*Above 50%*	*Below 50%*
Economic	Less than a day	83.3	16.7
	1-5 days	72.8	27.2
Personnel	Less than a day	81.4	18.6
	1-5 days	51.4	48.6
Other Issues	Less than a day	80.0	20.0
	1-5 days	42.8	57.2

UNIONS AND STRIKES

Labour management relationship is based on what the sociologist call "antagonistic co-operation". So, conflict is inevitable. The capitalist class intended to achieve maximum gains and benefits out of their capital invested in an industrial establishment even at the cost of labour class and on the other hand the labour class intended to remove socio-economic inequalities and protected its interests by avoiding conditions of exploitation. But removal of socio-economic inequalities pre- supposes a change in industrial relations. Trade Unionism has been a movement launched to bring this change.

The history of trade union movement all over the world illustrates the role of trade unions in the struggle for recognition and the right to exercise restrictive practices like strikes, boycotts, etc. against the philosophy of hire and fire.

The primary function of trade unions is the protection of socio-economic interest of the working class. To protect these interests, strike is used as a weapon in the hands of trade unions.

In Chapter III it has been stated that Unionism started lately in Orissa because of late start of industrialization. Earlier, analysis has also established link between unionisation and strike activity. Present analysis intends to provide an insight into the ideologies of Central Trade Union Organisations towards strike and their influence on strike activity in Orissa. Secondly it is also proposed to examine whether all the strikes are sponsored by the unions or sometimes work groups also resort to strike without the prior approval of the unions.

THE CENTRAL TRADE UNIONS

At present there are nine Central Trade Unions in India. Besides these, there are registered federations of unions in various industries and occupations. These federations are not affiliated to any central body, such federations are: The All India Bank Employees' Association, The National Federation of Indian Railwaymen, the All India Port and Dock Workers' Federation, the National Federation of Post and Telegraph, the All India Mine Workers' Federation, the Indian Federation of Working Journalists etc.

Details of the nine central trade unions are given in the table 5.13.

Besides the above, the Confederation of Free Trade Unions (C.F.T.U.) was formed in 1962, with the active support of the Christian Trade Unions. The Labour Progressive Federation was formed by D.M.K., Madras, Bharatiya Kamgar Sena and Shiva Sena, Bombay.

Government has recognized four Central Organisations (I.N.T.U.C., A.I.T.U.C., H.M.S., U.T.U.C.) of workers for the purpose of representation at national and international conferences and for occasional consultations.

Although the general objective of these four organisations are the same namely to promote the economic, social, political and cultural; interests of workers, they differ on some fundamental principles based on political attitudes.

As regards the methods used for attaining the desired objectives, there are some differences. I.N.T.U.C. believe in the principle of peaceful settlement of disputes between labour and capital. It attaches greater importance to the "right to secure justice" than to the "right to strike". To. I.N.T.U.C. the strike is not to be resorted to in a light-hearted manner.

A.I.T.U.C. endeavours to "achieve these objectives through legitimate, peaceful and democratic methods such as legislation,

Table 5.13 Central Trade Union Organisation in India

Central Unions	Year of formation	Affiliations with political parties	No. of affiliated unions	No. of membership claimed	In which industries most prominent
1	2	3	4	5	6
1. I.N.T.U.C.	1948	Ruling Congress party wedded to Gandhian philosophy	1516	18,86,440	Textile and Hosiery Industries, Tea, Plantation Transport, Mining and Metalic Industry
2. National Labour Organisation	1970	Organisation Congress, Wedded to Gandhian Philosophy	167	2,31,031	—do—
3. A.I.T.U.C. All India Trade Union Congress)	1920	Communist	1080	3,44,746	Engineering, Petroleum Building and Construction, Plantation
4. C.I.T.U. (Centre of Indian Trade Unions)	1970	Communist Party (Marxist CPIM)	1474	3,31,031	—

	Central Unions	Year of formation	Affiliations with political parties	No. of affiliated unions	No. of membership claimed	In which industries most prominent
	1	2	3	4	5	6
5.	U.T.U.C. (United Trade Union Congress) at Lennin Sarani Calcutta	1971/72	Radical Parties	112	1,17,031	Agriculture Ports docks Shipping Post and Telegraphs, Textile Plantation
6.	U.T.U.C. at Central Avenue, Calcutta	1971/72	—do—	158	35,384	—
7.	H.M.S. (Hind Mazdoor Sabha)	1948	Praja	364	4,51,167	Transport, Mining, Port and Docks Textiles, Plantation, Sugar, Iron and Steel
8.	H.M.P. (Hind Mazdoor Panchayat)		Samyukta Socialist Party			
9.	B.M.S. (Bharatiya Mazdoor Sangh)	1954	Jan Sangh		9,59,763	Textile, Sugar, Engineering, Shop Commerce

Source : Membership compiled from the "SHRAMIKA", May, 1984, Page 2.

education, propaganda, mass meetings, negotiation, demonstrations and in the last resort by strikes and similar methods as may be decided from time to time.

H.M.S. subscribe to the Marxist view of class struggle, but the focus is more on peaceful, legitimate and democratic methods i.e. on constitutional means, the right to strike is insisted upon.

U.T.U.C. believes that strike is to be declared as the last resort.

For the furtherance and realisation of the aims and objectives the B.M.S. employs all legitimate means consistent with spirit of nationalism.

National Front of Indian Trade Unions founded in 1967 places emphasis on certain "spiritual" values but rejects politicalisation of the trade unions.

Almost all the central organisations have their affiliated unions in Orissa. Table below shows the distribution of unions in Orissa according to their affiliation with the central organisations.

Table 5.14. Number of Trade Unions according to Central Affiliations (1976-85)

Year	*INTUC*	*AITUC*	*HMS*	*BMS*	*CITU*	*UTUC (IS)*	*Independent and Others*
1976	54	40	20	6	8	7	356
1977	46	35	17	8	6	7	391
1978	38	32	16	8	11	7	423
1979	40	30	15	11	21	9	427
1980	43	37	18	11	27	9	526
1985	51	53	35	14	41	9	716

Source : Hand book of Orissa Labour Statistics, 1981 and 1987 published by the Labour Commissioner, Orissa

This table shows that majority of unions are not affiliated to any central organisation. The number of independent unions is increasing at a faster rate than the affiliated unions.

Size of the unions according to their affiliation would reveal which organisaton has more influence in Orissa. Table 5.15

shows the distribution of unions according to their size and affiliation.

Table 5.15. Average Membership of Unions according to their Affiliation.

Year	*INTUC*	*AITUC*	*HMS*	*BMS*	*CITU*	*UTUC*	*Independent and Others*
1976	942	868	1332	453	510	1821	210
1977	1145	1068	1509	398	605	1920	211
1978	935	1152	1715	398	620	1949	302
1979	917	1303	1980	288	357	3489	280
1980	1078	1124	1847	775	369	3699	282
1985	1144	1136	1498	642	716	4081	509

Source : Hand book of Orissa Labour Statistics, published by the Labour Commissioner, Orissa.

The above table discloses that the average membership per union affiliated to U.T.U.C.was highest i.e. 2576 on average between 1976-80 and 4081 in 1985 per union and lowest for the independent unions. The unions affiliated to H.M.S. had the second highest position in average membership per union. I.N.T.U.C. and A.I.T.U.C. had 1003 and 1103 members per union respectively between 1976-80. But the number of unions affiliated to those two organisations were more in comparison to other unions.

INFLUENCE OF UNIONS ON STRIKE ACTIVITY

No doubt, unions have raised the status of workers all over the world. The workers raised their voice against their employer through unions. They struggled hard to obtain the right to strike. It is easier for the workers to use the weapon of strike through the unions. The problems of unionism like multiplicity of unions, trade union rivalry, leadership, politicisation of trade unions, problem of recognition, finance have changed the attitude of workers towards unions. Sometimes the workers are loosing their faith on the unions. The unions in certain circumstances ignore group, departmental and individual grievances. The union leaders sometimes act according to the wishes of the management and do not look into the workers' interest. Therefore at times workers declare strikes without the consent of unions.

In Orissa, the strike record shows that workers resort to strike even if they do not get the support of unions. The table below shows the percentage distribution of strikes declared by the unions and work-groups.

Table 5.16. Percentage Distribution of Strikes Declared by Unions and Work Groups

Period	*Percentage of Strikes*	
	Declared by Unions	*Declared by Work-groups*
1964-70	57.3	42.7
1971-80	59.2	40.8
1981-88	40.7	59.3

Source: The Labour Directorate, Government of Orissa.

The table above discloses that during 1964-70 out of 197 strikes, 113 were declared by the unions which was roughly 57 per cent of the total strikes declared during the period. 43 per cent of strikes were declared by the work-groups.

During 1971-80 roughly 59 per cent of the strikes were declared by the unions and 41 per cent by the work-groups. Between 1964 and 1980, out of 800 strikes, 470 were declared by the unions which was roughly 59 per cent of the total strikes. This shows that in comparison to sixties more strikes were declared by the unions during seventies. Between 1981-88, roughly 41 per cent of strikes are declared by unions and 59 per cent by the work group themselves. This shows that workers are becoming self dependent and developing faith on their own strength to fulfil their objectives.

Further analysis reveals that out of 470 strikes declared with the support of union, 214 strikes were declared by the independent unions. Among affiliated unions H.M.S. declared maximum number of strikes. Roughly 60 per cent of strikes were declared by the independent unions. The unions affiliated to H.M.S. contributed roughly 25 per cent of the strikes. The U.T.U.C. and I.N.T.U.C. affiliated unions, each shared 4 per cent of the strikes. Table 5.17

shows the percentage distribution of strikes declared by different unions.

Table 5.17. Percentage Distribution of Strikes by Unions according to their Affiliation between 1971 and 1980

Unions Affiliation	*Number*	*Percentage*
I.N.T.U.C.	16	4.4
A.I.T.U.C.	13	3.6
H.M.S.	88	24.6
B.M.S.	5	1.4
C.I.T.U.	5	1.4
U.T.U.C.	16	4.4
Independent and others	214	59.9

Source: The Labour Directorate, Government of Orissa.

In Orissa roughly 60 per cent of the strikes were declared by the unions and 40 per cent by the work groups. Among the strikes declared by the unions, 60 per cent accounted for the independent unions.

The possible explanation of why majority of strikes were declared by the independent unions is that majority of unions were not affiliated unions. The average size of independent unions showed that almost all the unions belonged to small sized organisations. They were newly formed unions and were increasing at a very fast rate. Earlier, analysis also showed that each year small sized organisations were added to the factory list.

TERMINATION OF STRIKES

In industry the class of employers and employees have contradictory and conflicting claims and interests. In such a state of affairs, struggles and frictions of these classes are bound to occur. In order to regulate the relations and struggles of these classes there must be some agency or instrumentality. At present, law is the most effective instrument through which Government regulates relations between employers and employees.

Throughout the world, the role of Government is a major variable in the labour-management relations field. Government intervenes in the employer-union relationship either to encourage, regulate or enforce the acceptance of its policy.

In India, Government directly regulates industrial relations as the employer in public sector undertakings and imposes restrictions on both the labour and management through legislative enactments in private sector undertakings. The Industrial Disputes Act of 1947, the Industrial Employment (Standing Orders) Act of 1946 and the Indian Trade Union Act of 1926 with their amendments and modifications provide the main legislative framework for regulating labour-management relationship in India.[12]

The Industrial Act of 1947 is the main instrument of State intervention. The primary objective of the Industrial Disputes Act as observed by the Supreme Court are "(1) the promotion of measures for securing and preserving amity and good relations between employer and workmen; (2) an investigation and settlement of industrial disputes between employers and employees, employers and workmen, with a right of representation by a registered trade union or association of employers or a federation of associations; (3) prevention of illegal strikes and lock-outs; (4) relief to workmen in the matter of lay-off and retrenchment; (5) collective bargaining."

Section 3(1) (2) of the Industrial Disputes Act provides for the setting up of Works Committee consisting of representatives of management and employers, in every undertaking employing hundred or more workmen, to promote measures, for security amity and good relations between employer and the workmen. Industrial relations will be most enduring, when it is founded on voluntary settlement, and it is hoped that the Works Committees will render recourse, to remaining machinery for the settlement of infrequent disputes.

The present machinery for the settlement of industrial disputes comprises: (i) conciliation (ii) arbitration (iii) adjudication machinery-tribunals, industrial courts, etc. The Act empowers the appropriate Government to appoint conciliation officers and/or constitute boards of conciliation to mediate in and promote settlement of industrial disputes. It also empowers the appropriate Government to refer disputes for adjudication by an industrial tribunal. The Act makes a distinction between disputes arising in public utility services and those in other industries and provides for compulsory conciliation and adjudication to resolve the former. Besides, the appropriate Government could constitute a court of enquiry to enquire into matters pertaining to an industrial dispute. Restrictions are placed on strikes/lock-outs in public utility services, and during the pendency of conciliation and adjudication proceedings. The details about the restrictions on strike and lock-outs have been discussed in Chapter II of the report. The procedure and machinery provided under the Act have been modified from time to time in the light of the actual working of these provisions, the decisions of the judiciary and the influence of the bipartite and tripartite agreements.

The aim of conciliation under Industrial Disputes Act is to bring about a settlement in disputes through third party intervention. Time limits are set to expedite conciliation proceedings before a conciliation officer within 14 days and two months before a conciliation board. A settlement arrived at in conciliation will be binding on the parties till such time, that is agreed upon between the parties and where no period is agreed upon, for a period of one year and will continue to be binding until revoked by a two months' notice by either party to the dispute.

The ultimate legal remedy for the settlement of an unresolved dispute is its reference to adjudication by the appropriate Government. The Industrial Disputes Act 1947, empowers the appropriate Government to constitute a labour court, industrial tribunal or national tribunal to adjudicate in a dispute.

A reference to an industrial tribunal will lie, where both the parties to an industrial dispute apply for such reference and also where the appropriate Government considers expedient to do so. An award of the tribunal may be enforced either wholly or in part, by the appropriate government for a period not exceeding one year. The power to refer disputes to industrial tribunals and enforce their awards is an essential corollary to the obligation that lies on the Government to secure conclusive determination of the disputes with a view to redressing the legitimate grievances of the parties.

The Industrial Disputes Act (section 10-A) makes provision for joint reference of industrial disputes to voluntary arbitration.

In Chapter III it has been discussed that in Orissa Government machinery is playing an effective role in settling industrial disputes. This analysis would examine how the strikes are terminated and what role is played by the Government. The table below gives the percentage distribution of strikes resolved through negotiation, conciliation and adjudication between 1964 and 1980.

Table 5.18. Percentage Distribution of Strikes resolved through negotiation, conciliation and adjudication between 1964 and 1980

Period	*Negotiation*	*Conciliation*	*Adjudication*
1964-70	29.9	54.3	15.2
1971-80	14.7	81.7	3.5

Source: The Labour Directorate, Government of Orissa.

The above analysis shows that during 1964-70 roughly 30 per cent of the total strikes were terminated through negotiation, 54 per cent through conciliation and 16 per cent referred to adjudication. Between 1971-80, roughly 15 per cent strikes were resolved through mutual discussion, 82 per cent of the strikes resolved through conciliation and only 3.5 per cent referred to adjudication.

This analysis discloses that conciliation machinery is playing an effective role in settlement of strikes. But bipartite negotiation is not encouraging. In comparison to 1960's the percentage of negotiation has decreased by 15 per cent and conciliation has increased by 27 per cent during 1970's. This shows that both the management and labour had developed a conciliatory approach towards industrial conflict but lack in developing a spirit of cooperation. This trend emerges because of the various problems, the trade unions are facing to-day. Multiplicity of trade unions and trade union rivalry stand on the way of mutual discussion and settlement of industrial disputes. To avoid the problem of union rivalry both the parties are referring to sign the agreement in the presence of conciliation officer even if they are able to settle the issue through negotiation.

SUMMARY

The following are the main points of the chapter:

1. In Orissa electricity, transport, machine making are highly strike-prone and iron and steel, basic metals, etc. are low strike-prone industries.
2. The annual average duration of strike decreased from 15.7 days to 8.1 days between 1966 and 1980.
3. More than 60 per cent of strikes are resolved within 5 days.
4. Roughly 60 per cent of the strikes are declared by the unions.
5. Majority of strikes are resolved through conciliation machinery.

CONCLUSIONS

A strike is a complex phenomenon. Strikes do not just happen. The occurrence of any strike action depends upon the actors involved in the situation. A number of factors like socio- economic environment, form of political integration, institutions of collective bargaining, management and trade union organisations have some relevance to the probability of strike action. In themselves these factors cannot explain the whole phenomenon of strikes. In many respects proposals for strikes are common under different industrial conditions. But one can observe marked differences in the pattern of strike activity in different countries, depending upon the differences in the influencing factors discussed above.

Most of the studies have concentrated upon the distribution of strikes between the countries, industries, plants or work groups. They are concerned with the conditions under which strikes are likely to occur. They emphasize the role of organisational and institutional factors in determining strike patterns. For example Ross and Hartman (1960) put emphasis on organisational factors, Kerr-Siegel's (1954) thesis accepted isolated homogeneous mass of workers as the source of strike activity. The work of Ashenfelter and Johnson (1969) is the first attempt at a complete incorporation of strike into a bargaining model. Vanderkamp argues that strike activity and economic activity tend to be positively related. In this inter-industry analysis, Shorey found that economic determinants are the important explanatory variables of stoppage frequency. The work of Shorter and Tilly indicates that strike-proneness is greater in the metropolitan areas where workers can meet more easily, communicate swiftly and can be certain that the demonstrations will have considerable impact on the public.

The above mentioned studies and a few others discussed in Chapter 2 of this report assigned economic and non-economic reasons to explain the nature of strike activity. Many others have shed light on the reasons for variations in strike pattern over the time, the mobilization of strike patterns, etc.

Strike activity being influenced by socio-economic and political factors, each industrial environment might serve to provide an insight into the nature of strike action. The research which is set out in this report provides an opportunity to study strikes in an industrially backward environment. The findings of the study reveal many interesting features of strike activity in a relatively economically backward region.

The discussions in the earlier chapters suggest many interesting and significant conclusions. Throughout the report it has been stressed that strike is an expression of conflict. The literature on the subject suggests that many factors are relevant for the occurrence of strikes. Strikes are seen as a means of achieving a more or less specified goal. To achieve that goal workers have to make a cautious approach to strike. They have to see the rationale for and against strike action. The first concern is the legitimacy of the demand. Secondly they have to estimate the chances of success. Thirdly they have to evaluate the organisational conditions which are basic for strike action.

The present study has not covered the socio-psychological aspect of strike action to draw any conclusions on the mobilization of strike action, the behaviour of strikers during the strike period and the after effects of a strike on workers.

This study has covered a number of detailed analysis on trends in strikes, causes of strikes, impact of plant size on strikes, role of the unions, the role of the Government, strikers-participation, etc. The findings of the analysis provide convincing support to substantiate conclusions on the following aspects of strike activity.

TRENDS IN STRIKES

The findings of the study discussed in Chapter 3 reveal that strikes in Orissa have an undeniable tendency to increase over the years. Ross and Hartman's contention that 'strikes are withering away' is found to be unacceptable. The results set out in this report illustrate that strikes are increasing in the terms of frequency, workers involvement and man-days lost. Man- days lost figures show a higher rate of increase in comparison to workers' involvement and number of strikes. Though, the frequency of strikes shows a decreasing trend after 1976, it cannot be a basis for future prediction as a continuous increasing trend is noticed in case of man-days lost.

The frequency of strikes and the number of workers involved and man-days lost are increasing at a faster rate in Orissa in comparison to figures for India as a whole.

In spite of increasing trend in frequency of strike, roughly 96 per cent of plants in Orissa are free from strike activity. Only 4 per cent of plants are affected by strikes. As such, this rising trend of strike frequency does not pose at the present, any serious threat to the industrial relations situation in the State, especially when considered in terms of their duration and participation rate. It has been analysed in chapter 6 that duration of strikes over the period 1966-89, has declined from 15.7 days to 6.6 days.

The State, under the leadership of the present government has embarked on an ambitious plan of economic growth. The rapid industrialisation of the State will further intensify the problems of multiplicity of unions, fractionalism and inter and intra-union rivalry in the State. Our analysis has shown that most of the large plants are multi-union plants, and multi-union plants are more prone to strike than single union plants. Keeping these things in view, one may draw the conclusion that unless the present trend of strike frequency is curbed through appropriate measures, it may, in future pose a threat, and upset the ambitious plan of industrialization of the State.

THE PARTIES AND THE RULES

Strikes are a most dramatic and fascinating aspect of industrial relations and directly affect the public. In the words of Lester:

> The community as a whole has an interest in industrial relations and labour disputes. Strikes and lock-outs may inconvenience many persons by stopping the flow of essential services such as transportation and electricity or of essential commodities like food and fuel. Work stoppages may also cause the whole community to suffer a large economic loss, while an accompanying boycott may result in economic injury to persons or firms not directly involved in the disputes. Presumably the government should afford some protection to third parties and prevent the dispute from degenerating into industrial anarchy.[1]

The mode of governmental intervention, however, differs from one country to another, depending on the political set up and the strength of the labour movement.

The discussions in the earlier chapters reveal that government is playing an effective role in regulating strike action. Too much intervention of the government machinery in the settlement of industrial disputes acts as a negative force on collective bargaining. In industrial relations a third party intervention is not a healthy sign of industrial peace. The weak bargaining position of workers, political orientation of trade unions, intra-union rivalry, lack of initiative of the management as well as of the union leaders to hold mutual discussions, all these compel the government machinery to step in.

An active intervention of the government machinery in resolving strikes or settlement of industrial disputes is not the solution of the problem. In order that the parties to the dispute might be encouraged into entering voluntary collective bargaining, the existing legislations governing industrial relations viz. the Industrial Disputes Act, 1947, the Trade Unions Act, 1926 and the Industrial Employment (Standing Orders) Act, 1946 need to be amended. The process of law is a continuous one. To regulate industrial action, the provisions of these laws require an improvement from time to time.

The recommendations of the National Commission on Labour (1969) for the creation of an Industrial Relations Commission and for a statutory recognition of trade unions are very important factors for maintaining harmonious relations between labour and management. In order to check a multiplicity of unions, membership requirement for the registration of trade unions need to be codified. The undue influence of outside leadership on trade unions is a major cause of weak trade unionism. This is to be corrected through statutory provisions.

However, the Central Government introduced three important industrial relations Bills in the year 1982. The Industrial Disputes Amendment Act 1982 contains very important provisions for speeding up the disposal of industrial disputes as well as enabling the Government to take action against unfair labour practices of both employers and employees. The Government has made it obligatory for employers having more than 50 workers in their organisation to set up Grievance Redressal Committees where an effort would be made at bipartite settlement of disputes between employers and workmen as soon as any problem arises. The conciliation machinery has been given greater power in order to summon parties to discussion and demand the production of documents.

The Trade Unions (Amendment) Bill, 1982 has made an attempt to lay down certain broad guide lines for the functioning of the trade unions. The Government would have greater power to verify the membership of trade union organisations. Trade unions can only be formed by registration by the workers themselves. A minimum of 10 per cent subject to 100 workers in an industry would be able in future to form a trade union. The percentage of outsiders as office bearers of trade unions is also proposed to be reduced from 50 to 25 per cent. The Bill has taken a significant step for the solution of inter-union and intra-union disputes.

The Industrial Employment (Standing orders) Act, 1947 was also amended in 1981. It seeks to give better service conditions to workmen.

The proposed legislation viz. The Trade Union and Industrial Relations Amendment Bill which was passed by the Rajya Sabha in May 1988 makes re-definition for certain terms. It also incorporates some of the recommendations of National Commission on Labour. The present amendment aims at the thought of the earlier bills, what could not be brought into force in 1979 and 1982 has been done in a different form. The proposed changes by the Government, it is felt will have a major impact in the entire working class. But this Bill has become a subject of controversy between the Government and the Trade Unions.

Besides, statutory provisions the employers and unions should adopt a positive strategy towards the day-to-day regulation of industrial relations. To be effective, the management requires powerful representatives as well as powerful trade unions. On the other hand unions should develop a co-operative attitude to facilitate fruitful negotiations.

FUTURE TREND

There may not be any decline in the trend of strike frequency in near future. It might on the other hand show an increasing trend. The economic and job conditions issues would continue to be the causative factors behind strike activity. Similarly bipartite settlement of industrial disputes may not be possible in the immediate future as any foreseeable change is not expected either in the attitude of the management or in the structure of unions. But with the increasing professionalisation of management, and better regulation of the economic and personnel issues by the state, strike in distant future, might become redundant, as has happened in some of the economically developed countries. This trend is gradually emerging also in Orissa as may be observed from the declining duration of strikes.

BIBLIOGRAPHY

BOOKS

ALEXANDER, K.W.J. AND JENKINS, C.L., FAIRFIELDS. A study of industrial change. London: Allen Lane, 1970.

ALLEN, V.L. Power in Trade Unions. London: Longmans, 1954.

ALLEN, V.L. Militant Trade Unionism. London: Merline Press, 1966.

ARYA, V.P. Strikes, Lock-outs and Gheraos: Law and Practices. Bombay: Oxford and IBH Publishing Co., 1967.

BATSTONE, ERIC, BORASTON IAN, FRENKEL STEPHEN. The Social Organisation of Strikes. Oxford: Blackwell, 1978.

BANNES, G.N. Industrial Conflicts, the way out, A study of the industrial problem in its practical aspects. London: Pitman, 1924.

BUGHANAN, D.M. Development of Capitalistic Enterprise in India. The Macmillan, 1934.

BAER, E. WALTER. Strikes: A study of conflict and how to resolve it. New York. Amacom, 1975.

BARNES, G.N. Industrial Conflicts: the way out. A Study of the Industrial Problems in its Practical Aspects. London: Pitman, 1924.

CHAKRABORTY P. (Mrs.). Strikes and Morale in Industry: in India and Her Principal States, New Delhi : Navan Printing Works Pvt. Ltd., 1969.

CLEGG, H.A. The System of Industrial Relations in Great Britain. Oxford: Blackwell, 1970.

COLE, G.D.H. The World of Labour. London: Bell, 1913.

CLELAND S. The influence of Plant Size on Industrial Relations. Princeton: Princeton University Press, 1955.

CLEGG, H.A. Trade Unionism under collective bargaining. Oxford: Blackwell, 1976.

COLE, G.D.H. An Introduction to British Trade Unionism. London: Allen and Unwin Ltd., 1953.

CHILD, J. Organization: A choice for Man. London: Allen and Unwin, 1973.

CLEGG, S. Power, Rule and Domination, Routledge and Kegan Paul. London.

CHAMBERLAIN N. W. and KUHN J.W. Collective Bargaining. McGraw- Hill, New York: 1965.

CHAMBERLAIN, N.W. AND SCHILLINGS S.M. The Impact of Strikes: Their Social and Economic Costs. New York: Harper, 1954.

CLEGG, H.A. and ADAMS. R. The Employers' Challenge. Oxford: Blackwell, 1957.

COATES, K. and TOPHAM, A. Industrial Democracy, London: Panther, 1970.

DAHRENDORF, R. Class and Class Conflict in an Industrial Society. Routledge and Kegan Paul, 1959.

DURKHEIM, EMILE. The Division of Labour in Society. Glencoe: Free Press, 1964.

DUNLOP, J.T. Industrial Relations Systems. Holt, 1958.

DUNNETTE, M.E. and KIRCHNER W.K. Psychology Applied to Industry. New York: Appleton-Century-Crofts. 1965.

DULLES, RHEAFOSTER. Labour in America: A History. New York: Vail- Ballou Inc., 1967.

DUNLOP, J.T. and CHAMBERLAIN, N.W. Frontiers of Collective Bargaining. New York: Harper and Row, 1967.

DAYAL, ISHWAR and SHARMA, B.A. Strikes of Supervisory Staff in the State Bank of India, Bombay: Progressive Corporation, 1971.

DUFTY, N.F. Industrial Relations in India. Bombay: Asia Publishing House, 1962.

EVANS, E.W. and CRIEGH, S.W. Industrial Conflict in Britain. London: Frank cases, 1977.

ELDRIDGE, J.E.T. (ed). Industrial Disputes, Routledge and Kegan Paul, 1968.

FLANDERS ALLAN. Trade Unions. London: Hutchinson, 1968.

FLANDERS, A. (ed). Collective Bargaining. Harmondsworth: Penguin, 1969.

FLANDERS, A. Management and Unions. London: Faber and Faber, 1970.

FOX, A.A. Sociology of Work in Industry. London: Collier- Macmillan, 1971.

FROW, R., FROW E. and KATANKA, M. Strikes A Documentary, History. London: Charles Knight, 1971.

GOULDNER, A.W. Wildeat Strike. Broad House. Carter Lane: Routledge and Kegan Paul, 1955.

GIRI, V.V. Labour Problems in Indian Industries: Bombay: Asia Publishing House, 1962.

GOLDTHORPE, J.H. LOCK WOOD, D. BECHOFOR F. and PLATT, J. The Affluent Worker: Industrial Attitudes and Behaviour. Cambridge University Press, 1968.

GALENSON, WALTER. Trade Union Democracy in Western Europe. Berkeley: University of California Press, 1962.

GOODMAN, J.F.B. and WHITTINGHAM, T.G. Shop Stewards in British Industry, London: McGraw-Hill, 1969.

HAWKINS, K. Conflict and Change. Aspects of Industrial Relations. New York: Holt, 1972.

HYMAN, R. Strikes. London: Fontana, 1972.

HERLING, JOHN, Labour Unions in America. Bombay: Vora Publishing Pvt. Ltd., 1970.

INGHAM, GEOFFREY K. Strikes and Industrial Conflict in Britain and Scandinavia. London: Macmillan, 1974.

JOHRI, C.K. Unionism in a Developing Economy.

JOSHI, N.M. Trade Union Movement in India. Bombay: Longman Green & Co., 1927.

KESSLER, SIDNEY AND WEEKS, BRIAN. Conflict at Work: Reshaping Industrial Relations (ed.). London: British Broad Casting Corporation, Trinity Press, 1971.

KOTHARI, M. GANPATLAL. A Study of Industrial Law. Bombay: C. Jamnadas & Co., 1968.

KARNIK, V.B. Strikes in India. Bombay: Manaktalas, 1967.

KNOWLES, K.G.J.C. Strikes : A Study in Industrial Conflict. Oxford, Blackwell, 1952.

KORNHAUSER, A., DUBIN R. and ROSS, A.M. (ed.). Industrial Conflict, New York: McGraw-Hill, 1954.

KHUN, JAMES W. Bargaining in Grievance Settlement. New York: Columbia, 1961.

KERR, C. Labour and Management in Industrial Society. New York: Harper, 1964.

KASSALOW, E.M. Trade Unions and Industrial Relations. An International Comparison. New York: Random House, 1969.

LEESON, R.A. (ed.). Strikes. London: Allen and Unwin. 1973.

MAMORIA, C.B. Dynamics of Industrial Relations in India. Bombay: Himalaya Publishing House, 1983.

MARSHALL, D. HOWARD and MARSHAL, J. NATALIE. Collective Bargaining. New York: Random House.

MATHUR, A.S. . and J.S. MATHUR. Trade Union Movement in India. Chaitanya Publishing House, Allahabad, 1957.

MATHUR, A.S. Labour Policy and Industrial Relations in India. Ram Prasad & Sons, Agra: 1958.

MICHAEL, V.P. Industrial Relations in India and Workers' Involvement in Management, Himalaya Publishing House, Bombay, 1979.

OWEN, W.V. and FINSTON, H.V. Industrial Relations: Management, Labour and Society, Appleton Century Crafts, New York: 1954.

PATIL, S. Conciliation in India: Its Functioning and Effectiveness, Chugh Publishers, Allahabad: 1977.

PIGOU, A.C. Economics of Welfare, Vol. II.

PIGOU, P. & OTHERS. Social Problems in Labour Relations, 1939.

PUNCKAR, S.D. Trade Unionism in India, New Book Company, Bombay, 1948.

PUNCKAR, S.D. Industrial Peace in India, Vora & Co., Bombay: 1952.

PETERSON, FLORENCE. American Labour Unions: What they are and how they work. Delhi: Sterling Publishers (P) Ltd. 1963.

RICHARDSON, J. HENRY. An Introduction to the Study of Industrial Relations, George Allen & Unwin, London: 1961.

ROBERTS, R.C. Trade Union in a Free Society. Hutchinson London: 1962.

ROBERTS, B.C. (ed.). Industrial Relations: Contemporary Problems and Perspectives, Asia Publishing House, Bombay: 1962.

ROBERTSON, N. THOMAS, J.L. Trade Unions and Industrial Relations, Business Books, London: 1968.

ROSS, A.M. and HARTMAN, P.T. Changing Patterns of Industrial Conflict, New York: Wiley, 1960.

RAMAN, RAO, A.V. Collective Bargaining Versus Government Regulation India and U.S.A. Calcutta: Allied Publishers Pvt. (Ltd.), 1964.

SMITH, C.T.B., CLIFTON RICHARD, MAKEHAM PETER, CRIIGH and BURNRV. Strikes in Britain, Manpower Paper No. 5, 1978.

SHORTER, EDWARD AND CHARLES, TILLY. Strikes in France, 1830-1968. Cambridge: Cambridge University Press, 1974.

TAYLOR, J. BENJAMIN and WITNEYFRED. Labour Relations Law. Englewood Cliffs, Prentice-Hall Inc., New Jersey: 1975.

TONDON, B.K. Collective Bargaining and the Indian Scene. Sultan Chand and Sons, Delhi: 1972.

TURNER, H.A. The Trend of Strikes. Leeds, Leeds University Press, 1963.

WEDDERBURN, K.W. The Worker and the Law. Harmondsworth, Penguin, 1971.

WIGHAM, E.L. What's wrong with the Union? Harmondsworth: Penguin, 1961.

JOURNALS

ANON. "Labour Dispute and Settlement in the United States Steel Industry". International Labour Review. Vol. 82 (1), July 1960. pp. 59-69.

ANON. "Industrial Disputes in India during 1961". Indian Labour Journal. Vol. 4(2), February 1963, pp. 135-161.

ASHENFELTER, O and PIERCE, W.S. Industrial Conflict: The Power of Prediction: A Comment on Dubin", Industrial and Labour Relations Review. Vol. 19(1), 1966, pp. 92.95.

ASHENFELTER, O and JOHNSON, G. "Bargaining Theory, Trade Unions, and Industrial Strike Activity". American Economic Review. Vol. 59(1), March 1969, pp. 35-49.

BLUMLER, J.G. and EWBANK, A.J. "Trade Unionists, the Mass Media and Unofficial Strikes". British Journal of Industrial Relations. Vol. 8(1), 1970. pp 32-54.

CAMERON, G.S. "Post-War Strikes in the North-East Ship- Building and Ship Repairing Industry, 1946-61". British Journal of Industrial Relations. Vol. 2(1). 1964, pp. 1-22.

CHAKRABORTY, P. "Forms and Trends of Industrial Unrest in W. Bengal". Indian Labour Journal. Vol 13(5), 1972.

CHAKRABORTY, P. "Closures, Lock-outs, Strikes. A Study of Workers' Reaction". Indian Journal of Industrial Relations. Vol. 9(2), 1973.

CHAMBERLAIN, N.W. "Strikes in Contemporary Context". Industrial and Labour Relations Review. Vol. 20(4), July 1967.

DAYAL, ISHWAR and SHARMA, B.A. "Strikes of Supervisory Staff in the State Bank of India", Bombay: Progressive Corporation, 1971.

DAYAL, ISHWAR, SRIVASTAVA, S. and ALFRED, T.M "Anatomy of a Strike". Bombay, Somaiya Publications, 1972.

DUBIN, R. "A Theory of Conflict and Power in Union Management Relations" Industrial and Labour Relations Review. Vol. 13, July 1960.

DUBIN, R. "Industrial Conflict-The Power of Prediction". Industrial and Labour Relations Review, Vol. 18, April 1965.

ELDRIDGE, J.E.T. and CAMERON, G.E. "Unofficial Strikes Some Objections Considered" British Journal of Sociology. Vol. 15(1), March 1964. pp. 11-30.

EVANS, E.W. and GALAMBOS, P. "Work stoppages in the U.K., 1951-64: A Quantitative Study", Bulletin of the Oxford Institute of Economics and Statistics. Vol. 28(1), 1966, pp. 38- 57.

EVANS, E.W. and GALAMBOS, P. "Work stoppages in the United Kingdom 1965-70". Bulletin of Economic Research. Vol. 25(1), 1973, pp. 22-43.

FORCHHEIMER, K. "Some International Aspects of the Strikes Development". Oxford Institute of Statistics-Bulletin, Vol. 10(1), 1948, pp. 9-18.

FOX, A. "Managerial Ideology and Labour Relations". British Journal of Industrial Relations. Vol. 4, 1966, pp. 366- 378.

GALAMBOS, P. and EVANS, E.W. "Work-stoppages in the United Kingdom, 1951-1964". A Quantitative Study . Bulletin of the Oxford University Institute of Economics and Statistics, Vol. 28(1), 1966, pp. 33-58.

GALAMBOS, P. and EVANS E.W. "Work-stoppages in United Kingdom, 1951-64: A Reply". Bulletin of the Oxford Institute of Economic and Statistics. Vol. 28(4), 1966, pp. 283-248

GOODMAN, J.F.B. "Strikes in the United Kingdom-Recent Statistics and Trends". International Labour Review Vol. 95(5), May 1967, pp. 465-481.

JURKAT, E.H. and JURKAT, D.B. "The Economic Function of Strikes" Industrial & Labour Relations Review, Vol. 2(4), 1949. pp. 527-545.

KASSALOW, E.M. Trade Unions and Industrial Relations. An International Comparison. New York, Random House, 1969.

KERR, C. and SIEGEL, A. Inter-industry Propensity to Strike in Flanders, A. (ed.). Collective Bargaining. Harmondsworth, Penguin, 1969.

KNOWLES, K.G.J.C. "Strikes and their Changing Economic Context" Bulletin of the Oxford Institute of Statistics. Vol. 9(2), 1947, pp. 287-306.

KNOWLES, K.G.J.C. "Strike-Proneness and its Determinants", American Journal of Sociology. Vol. 60 (3), Nov. 1954, pp. 213-229.

KNOWLES, K.G.J.C. "Work Stoppages in the United Kingdom: A Comment," Bulletin of the Oxford Institute of Economic and Statistics, Vol. 28(1), 1966 pp. 59-62.

LEEVITT, THEODORE, Prosperity Verses Strikes. Industrial and Labour Relations Review. Vol. VI, 1953 pp. 220-226.

LYNCH, LISA. "Strike Frequency in British Coal Mining 1950-1974" British Journal of Industrial Relations, Vol. XVI(1), 1978. pp. 95-98.

OXNAM, D.W. "International Comparisons of Industrial Conflict" Journal of Industrial Relations (Sydney) Vol. 7(1) . 1965. pp. 144-163.

OXNAM, D.W. "Issues in Industrial Conflict-An International Comparison", Journal of Industrial Relations (Sydney) Vol. 13(2) 1971.

PANDEY, S.M. and PATHAK V.K. "Inter-Industry Conflict Proneness in India" Indian Journal of Industrial Relations. Vol. 7(4) 1972. pp. 521-534.

PETERSON, T.T. and WILLETT F.J. "Unofficial Strike". Sociological Review. Vol. 43(1) 1957.

REES, A. Industrial Conflict and Business Fluctuations. Journal of Political Economy. Vol. 60, Oct. 1952. pp. 371-82..

PERIODICALS

The Economic Times, Bombay.

The Economic and Political Weekly, Bombay.

Yojna, New Delhi.

Industrial Times, Bombay.

Industrial and Labour Relations Review.

Indian Journal of Industrial Relations, Sri Ram Centre for Industrial Relations, New Delhi.

Indian Journal of Labour Economics, Indian Society of Labour, Lucknow.

International Labour Review, Geneva.

The Indian Worker, Indian National Trade Union Congress, New Delhi.

Labour Information Service, Indian National Trade Union Congress, New Delhi.

GOVERNMENT DOCUMENTS AND PUBLICATIONS

Government of India, Report of the Royal Commission on Labour, 1931.

Government of India, Report of the National Commission on Labour, 1969.

MINISTRY OF LABOUR AND EMPLOYMENT, LABOUR BUREAU, GOVERNMENT OF INDIA, SIMLA

Indian Labour Journal.
Indian Labour Gazette, Simla.
Indian Labour Statistics, New Delhi.
Indian Labour Year Book, Simla.
Year Books, etc.
India, New Delhi (various years)
Indian Labour Year Book, Simla (various years)
Indian Labour Statistics, Simla (various years)
I.L.O. Year Book (various years)

BUREAU OF STATISTICS AND ECONOMICS, ORISSA, BHUBANESWAR

Statistical Abstract of Orissa, 1977.
Statistical Abstract of Orissa, 1979.
Economic Survey of Orissa, 1980-81.

THE LABOUR COMMISSIONER, ORISSA, BHUBANESWAR

Orissa Labour News (various months)
Hand Book of Labour Statistics (various years)

BARE ACTS

The Trade Unions Act, 1926.
Industrial Employment (Standing Orders) Act, 1946.
Industrial Disputes Act, 1947.
Payment of Wages Act, 1936.
Minimum Wages Act, 1948.
Payment of Bonus Act, 1965.
Orissa Shops and Commercial Establishments Act, 1956.
Orissa Minimum Wages Rules, 1954.
British Industrial Relations Act, 1971.
Labour Management Relations Act, 1947.

Index